Curriculum Experiences
for Literacy, Learning, and Living

By: Kathy Staugler

Fall Fantasy

Transportation

School Is Cool

Community Helpers

This Is Me

Help At Home

Thanksgiving Dinner

Holiday Grooming

Forest Animals

Printed in the U.S.A.
Second Printing February 2001
Third Printing September 2004
Fourth Printing October 2008

Mayer-Johnson LLC
P.O. Box 1579
Solana Beach, CA 92075-7579
U.S.A.
Phone: 800-588-4548 or 858-550-0084
Fax: 858-550-0449
Email: mayerj@mayer-johnson.com
Web: www.mayer-johnson.com

ISBN 1-884135-39-0

About The Author

Kathy Staugler, M.A., CCC-SLP attended Ball State University in Muncie, Indiana where she received Bachelor's and Master's degrees in both Speech Pathology and Special Education. During her professional career, she has served as a public school speech pathologist, teacher of children with developmental handicaps, and communication specialist for children with multiple handicaps. Presently, Kathy consults with schools on the augmentative communication/assistive technology needs of students in a seven county region of West Central Ohio. She has presented regional workshops on adaptive strategies and techniques for special needs and inclusionary classroom settings.

Dedication

Special thanks to the many special educators in West Central Ohio who have shared their ideas which are reflected in these unit topics and activities.

Table Of Contents

Introduction

The Need for a Curriculum

In every educational program, a course of study is identified which outlines the scope of the educational learning experiences. Educators in similar grade or subject levels commonly collaborate to determine the skills that are expected for mastery. School districts then adopt these curriculum plans to assure direction to teachers, as well as continuity in the educational program as students progress through the years. Based on the adopted curriculum, school districts review and select materials that will facilitate learning of established curriculum goals.

Historically, the educational needs of children with multiple disabilities did not seem to fit into the scope of the regular curriculum adopted by a school district. Various alternate curriculums were developed in an attempt to meet specific areas of learning needs. These courses of study were often labeled as developmental, functional, or sensory. Academic subject matter was characteristically "watered down" or felt to be inappropriate for the student with disabilities.

Appropriate materials to utilize in these special educational settings were limited and teachers were often found creating their own. As students progressed from level to level, the focus of a classroom was likely to reflect the teacher's perspective of needed skills rather than a continuity that flowed into a level of proficiency.

Many children with disabilities are now being educated in regular education programs. Special educators are assigned the task of adapting and adjusting the curriculum to meet the individual needs of each child.

In instances of children with multiple handicapping needs, the content areas of the typical curriculum may advance to a level that exceeds lifetime applications that are needed for the student. It is then necessary to present alternate curriculum subject matter that will pertain to the needs of the child.

Whether children with multiple disabilities are being educated in the regular education setting, a resource room, or self-contained classroom, the focus of learning must be on providing a meaningful educational environment. The curriculum experiences of this book offer direction and guidelines for skills that will enable students to learn and live.

Philosophy

Children can learn if actively participating in the learning process. Literacy learning should be included for all children and does not imply that a certain set of "readiness" skills should be achieved prior to inclusion. The content of learning experiences should be relevant to the student's age, interest, and abilities. Educational curriculums should reflect an ongoing series of goals that will allow each individual to effectively control their own lives, successfully participate, and contribute to society.

These curriculum experiences are developed on that philosophy that:
- All children should be stimulated with literacy experiences.
- All children should be provided a means to actively interact with learning/language activities.
- Learning/language activities must be related to real life experiences within the child's environment.
- Learning must aim toward increased independence for the child.

The curriculum experiences presented in this book offer a progressive format for developing a program for students with multiple disabilities. It attempts to take into consideration the specialized needs of many children, with emphasis on the fact that not all will achieve the same level of mastery. The means in which students are involved in the curriculum is far more important than the activities of the curriculum.

Domains

The curriculum is divided into seven domains. The emphasis on each of these domains varies as the student progresses through school. These domains are:
- Literacy
- Communication
- Independent living
- Community living
- Recreation/Leisure
- Vocational
- Participation with typical peers

The curriculum promotes a whole learning approach. Aspects of each domain are incorporated throughout all educational activities. Each curriculum level includes graphs that highlight the emphasis placed on the seven domains for that particular level.

Literacy is defined as learning that provides opportunities to read, listen, speak, and write. Print forms include text, numbers, and symbolizations. The student's ability to communicate in all activities is essential. Direct instruction of literacy and communication are emphasized in the early levels, while application is stressed during the upper levels.

Each student should be provided the opportunity to interact with typically developing peers with a blend of classroom study and community experiences. This may vary according to the educational setting and age of the student. The educational team should define the extent and means for participation.

Independent living, community involvement, and recreational activities are critical learning aspects for application into adult life skills. Vocational preparation should be practical with realistic expectations for the individual. The end result of the curriculum should provide the student with a transition to adult living and employment.

Curriculum Levels

The intent of this curriculum is not to sequence skills developmentally, but to present goals and objectives that are important to independent functioning. Alternative strategies and techniques should be incorporated at each level to accommodate the special learning needs of the individuals. Curriculum levels are identified by students' ages and interests.

- Primary
- Elementary
- Intermediate
- Middle school
- Junior/Senior High
- Transition

Guidelines for Instructional Activities

Within each level are general guidelines. These may be applicable to setting up a special education classroom, or as adaptive techniques to be employed within regular educational settings. Symbolized materials are included for routine classroom activities. A sample of a weekly schedule is also included for each level. While these are more specifically designed for special education classroom and resource room settings, these are implications that may be applied to other educational environments.

Unit Topics

Nine unit topics are incorporated for each level of the curriculum. These provide the basis for activities and materials. Each topic takes into consideration the students' interests and age levels, with emphasis on application to daily living routines. Topics are intended to be incorporated over a one month period. This allows for repeated use and application of all learning skills. The skills practiced during the month topic should also follow over into application in future topics of learning. Each topic has the possibility of branching into additional skill areas and topics. When applicable, these topics should be included. The materials included in this book are not all-inclusive, but do serve as a framework for encompassing topics that flow in a progressive manner.

Checklist

A checklist of goals from the curriculum is provided for each topic. This checklist outlines the skills that should be presented during the unit. It may be used for reporting of the student's participation.

Parent Letter

Each unit includes a letter for parents. It is critical to keep the family informed of skills that are being introduced, taught, and practiced. Whenever possible, expand the learning from the school setting into the home environment.

The Story

A symbolized story is the focal point of each topic. Each story may be reproduced, colored, and constructed into durable format for repeated use. It is suggested that pages be placed in top loading page protectors, adding a sheet of tagboard for extra sturdiness. All pages can then be arranged in a ring binder. This provides a more easily accessible format for different motor abilities. Additional page modifications may be included, such as page fluffers, depending on the individual students in a classroom.

Active participation in story reading should be encouraged. This may include page turning, sentence completion, or pointing to symbols and pictures. Symbolized forms are included below the text of each story. This serves as an introduction to new symbols, or cues for reading.

A 3 x 3 overlay is incorporated to go along with the story topic. It may be utilized as a manual board, or integrated into other types of voice output systems that will give the students a means to interact in story reading.

Other input/output modes of languages may be added to enhance participation, i.e. manual, signs, or use of manipulative objects.

Story reading should occur on a regular basis during the unit, increasing participation throughout. Other books and stories with related topics should also be incorporated during the unit.

Worksheets

Worksheet formats have been included with each unit. These are intended to provide a sampling of activity ideas. These worksheets may be laminated or made more sturdy to use in repeated activities, center activities, or game playing activities. Again, it is important to modify accessibility to materials at the level of each student.

Communication

Throughout the unit, each student should have the means and opportunity to interact through various modes of communication. Nonverbal means, such as facial expressions, smiles, and eye pointing may be appropriate for some students. Single switch access to a tape recorder with a loop tape, or a BIGmack™ switch offer single message responses. Utilize the picture symbols from the unit for manual communication boards, or attach these with messages to devices. Throughout the units, it is advisable to consider all modes that a student can effectively use to increase participation. Keep a focus on what modes will take the student into the future as an active communicator.

Communication interactions should flow naturally in each lesson. Utilize open-ended question forms that provide the student with turn taking opportunities to offer information and comments. Pause after a communication is directed toward a student, anticipating a response. One of the most valuable tools we can teach our students is the ability to interact communicatively.

Role Playing

Many units lend themselves to role playing. Role playing situations serve as a practice for real-life experiences. This is particularly necessary when the student will be going into the community to apply learning during a unit. In the classroom, the supports and structured scripting will enable the student to feel more comfortable in the actual application.

Have Fun!

This book is designed to offer a sound framework for the educational program of students with multiple disabilities. It is in no way the "end" of skills and activities that can be presented. It should also not be considered a checklist for selecting IEP goals. It is simply a basis for the educational curriculum which set the direction for classroom management of practical learning situations.

Be creative! Keep a focus! And above all, enjoy the learning that is happening in your classroom.

Elementary Level: Overview

The elementary level book contains nine unit topics that are of interest to the second and third grade aged student. Each unit contains a reproducible story and related activities that can be integrated into monthly educational learning. The units integrate an academic and functional curriculum in a manner that prepares students for participation in the school, home, and community.

If acquisition of academic skills is possible, this is the time to see growth. Communication, fine motor skills, and learning tasks are encouraged in a normal developmental pattern. Within this pattern, adaptations will be refined to accommodate the specific needs of the child. By now it should be more evident if the child will be a verbal communicator, or if an augmentative system should be implemented. Mobility issues are addressed to enable maximum independence while traveling throughout the school facilities. Participation in programs with typically developing peers continues to be encouraged, with the opportunity to use adaptations within these settings.

Curriculum topics increase the child's awareness of his/her responsibilities in the home and community. Independent self-care in these activities can be learned through classroom experiences. Taking turns and interacting with fellow classmates become routine in these structured activities.

Elementary Level Emphasis

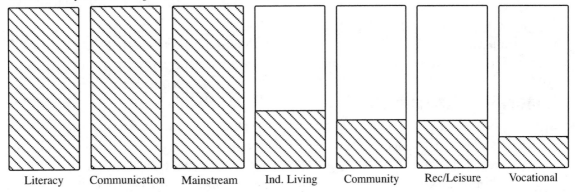

Literacy   Communication   Mainstream   Ind. Living   Community   Rec/Leisure   Vocational

Guidelines: Instructional Activities

Instructional activities covered in this unit include:

- Circle Time
- Centers
- Grooming
- Fine Motor Craft

- Unit Activities
- Directed Free Play
- Gross Motor Skills
- Snack Time

Circle Time

Circle time is a whole-class group lesson. Students participate in:

- Greetings
- Calendar
- Weather-related activities

The format of circle time should remain fairly consistent—a sequence of activities, songs, or routines that can be predicted. This is a period when students can learn to remain seated and attend to the present activity. Activities should remain fast moving with each student getting frequent opportunities to actively participate. Designating a bulletin board or chalkboard for circle time creates a focal point for the students and an easy way for teachers to organize materials. Velcro® or magnetic backing on cards provides a simple way to make daily changes in the activities.

For some students, the calendar and weather activities may not become a functional skill needed in their lives. However, the group interaction will provide opportunity for routine participation.

Morning Greetings

Starting the day with greetings gives the students a structured way to learn social rituals and interact with other students. This should be a fast moving activity, including simple greetings and "How are you?" interactions. If students have information to share from home, this may serve as a time to allow comments. Nonverbal students may employ a tape recorder for messages from home.

Daily Attendance

Using name or photo cards with students' names will provide a quick manner to take attendance while the students learn to read others' names. Expand the activity by counting how many boys or girls are present and how many students are absent.

Calendar and Weather

Students should become aware of the present day and yesterday. Typical calendars may be used for students to mark the day and identify the number and month. Talking about the weather is a typical conversational skill people use their whole life. This is a great opportunity to make comments, i.e. "Rainy days are yucky!"

Today's Menu

Picture cards may be used to identify the menu items for the day. This is a way to begin noticing food groups. Students may also make comments to express their likes and dislikes.

Unit Activities

Utilizing a whole-language approach, each unit includes a theme, a story, and related activities. Activities are holistic but can be identified in the areas of literacy (language arts and math), community and independent living, recreation/leisure, and vocational. A unit is designed to be incorporated for approximately one month. While the entire class is involved in the same monthly theme, the specific objectives may vary to meet individual needs.

Time periods for unit activities are best employed with small groups. The types of activities are varied: specific instructional lessons, story reading, songs, role playing, games, cooking, crafts, etc.

Centers

Center activities are reinforcement of unit activities that have been presented by the teacher. These are activities that students may accomplish with minimal adult supervision. Utilizing a teacher assistant during this time will assure that students are able to perform the tasks as expected.

Directed Free Play

Providing direction to free play periods assures that students learn to utilize toys and games appropriately, interact with others, and take turns. Students with limited mobility may also require adaptations and physical assistance to participate in these activities.

Grooming

Daily grooming routines should be started early, as a self-help skill and to establish good habits. Face washing, teeth brushing, and hair combing are skills that should be incorporated during this time. Adult supervision and assistance will vary with each individual child.

Gross Motor Skills

Designated periods should be set aside for specific gross motor development skills. The assistance of an adapted or regular P.E. teacher is often very beneficial. The physical therapist may also have suggestions for enabling motorically involved students to participate. There are simple ways to create an atmosphere during this lesson that relates to the monthly unit topic.

Fine Motor Craft

This may be a time period for coloring, cutting, or pasting. Or it may be an opportunity to create a simple craft project. Find a project that will relate to the monthly unit topic to reinforce the vocabulary. Occupational therapists and school art teachers often have suggestions for these activities.

Snack Time

Daily snack time provides nourishment before the student heads home, and also facilitates a relaxed group setting. Simple snacks may be prepared or treats may be brought in by students. This activity allows students the opportunity to pass out items one-to-one. It is a chance to reinforce those eating skills and table manners. This is a time when "please" and "thank you" can be reinforced.

Ideas: Reading/Spelling Activities

These reading/spelling activities may be utilized with vocabulary from any of the unit topics:

- Reading Bingo
- Board Games
- Hangman or Wheel of Fortune
- Pictures and Sentences
- Clues

- Go Fish
- Matching Game
- Mixed Up Sentences
- Spelling Activities

Reading Bingo

Use the unit vocabulary to create bingo boards on the Reading Bingo worksheet, page 7. Students will select words and glue them on the various squares. Play bingo in the usual manner with students matching the words or symbols that are called. Students may read the word, identify objects, use the word in a sentence, demonstrate the action, or use other associated concepts to demonstrate reading skills with the words.

Go Fish

Use the vocabulary cards (symbols/words) included with each unit to make a Go Fish game. Attach multiple sets to index cards. Students will play the game by asking another student for a card that will create a match. If the student does not have that card, he/she may tell the other student to "Go Fish" and select a card from the draw pile.

Board Games

Use the blank board game on page 8 to create a reading game:

- Add symbols/words to the spaces. Students roll the dice or spin a spinner to determine the number of spaces to move. Read each word along the path.

- Use cards with symbols/words as the draw cards. Put a number on each card. Students draw a card, read it, and then move the number of spaces listed on the card.

- Put letters on the spaces of the board game. Students roll the dice or spin a spinner to determine the number of spaces to move. They will identify the letter on the space they land on and name a word from the vocabulary cards that begins with that letter.

Matching Game

Create double sets of the vocabulary cards (symbols/words). Glue them onto index cards. Turn the cards face down. Students will select two cards and turn them over, reading the word on each card. When a match is located, the student is allowed to take another turn.

Hangman or Wheel of Fortune

Select a word or sentence with reading vocabulary. Write the sentence with blank spaces. Students will guess a letter, filling in the blank if the letter is in the word/sentence. Students may guess the word/sentence when they know it. Play the game similar to the rules of Hangman or Wheel of Fortune.

Mixed Up Sentences

Create a sentence using one or more of the vocabulary words. Cut apart the words and mix them up. Have the students rearrange them into a meaningful sentence. Read the sentences.

Pictures and Sentences

Take pictures of the students doing activities that display action with the vocabulary words, i.e. if one of the reading words is "read," take a picture of a student reading. Make sentence cards related to the pictures, e.g., "Jason will read a book." Students will match the sentence with the correct picture.

Spelling Activities

Students will reproduce the words using a variety of letter-by-letter modes:

■ Present the word — student will copy or type the word.

■ Present the word — student will select letters from a stamp pad set to "write" the word.

■ Present the word — student will cut out letters from a newspaper to match the letters of the word.

■ Present the word — student takes a turn naming the next letter. As a student names a letter, another student writes or types what is said. The last person will read the word.

Clues

Present three words from the vocabulary cards. Give a series of clues about one word. Students are to name the word described. For example:

read   book   eat

This word starts with a "b."
It has pages in it.
We find it in a library.
What is it?

Reading Bingo

Directions: Add picture symbols/words from a unit.

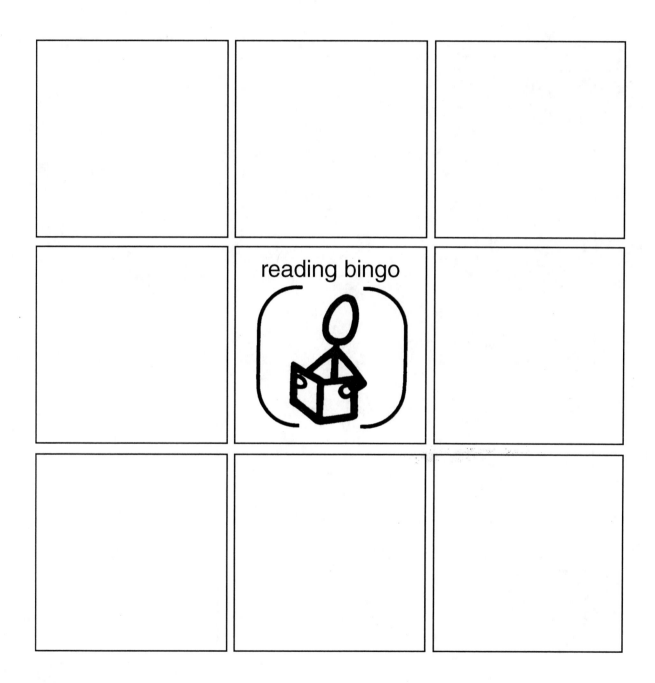

Board Game

start

STOP

Level: Elementary

Sample Weekly Schedule:
Elementary Level

*Activities in regular education programs may be scheduled appropriately for recommended students at periods throughout the day.

Monday	Tuesday	Wednesday	Thursday	Friday
8:30 - 9:00 Circle Time	8:30 - 9:00 Circle Time	8:30 - 9:00 Circle Time	8:30 - 9:00 Circle Time	8:30 - 9:00 Circle Time
9:00 - 9:15 Story Reading	9:00 - 9:15 Story Reading	9:00 - 9:15 Story Reading	9:00 - 9:15 Story Reading	9:00 - 9:15 Story Reading
9:15 - 10:00 Unit Activities/ Supervised Centers	9:15 - 10:00 Unit Activities/ Supervised Centers	9:15 - 10:00 Unit Activities/ Supervised Centers	9:15 - 10:00 Unit Activities/ Supervised Centers	9:15 - 10:00 Unit Activities/ Supervised Centers
10:00 - 10:30 Recess/Directed Free Play	10:00 - 10:30 Recess/Directed Free Play	10:00 - 10:30 Recess/Directed Free Play	10:00 - 10:30 Recess/Directed Free Play	10:00 - 10:30 Recess/Directed Free Play
10:30 - 11:15 Unit Activities/ Supervised Centers	10:30 - 11:15 Unit Activities/ Supervised Centers	10:30 - 11:15 Unit Activities/ Supervised Centers	10:30 - 11:15 Unit Activities/ Supervised Centers	10:30 - 11:15 Unit Activities/ Supervised Centers
11:15 - 11:30 Restrooming/ Prepare for lunch	11:15 - 11:30 Restrooming/ Prepare for lunch	11:15 - 11:30 Restrooming/ Prepare for lunch	11:15 - 11:30 Restrooming/ Prepare for lunch	11:15 - 11:30 Restrooming/ Prepare for lunch
11:30 - 12:30 Lunch Recess	11:30 - 12:30 Lunch Recess	11:30 - 12:30 Lunch Recess	11:30 - 12:30 Lunch Recess	11:30 - 12:30 Lunch Recess

Sample Weekly Schedule: Elementary Level

*Activities in regular education programs may be scheduled appropriately for recommended students at periods throughout the day.

Monday	Tuesday	Wednesday	Thursday	Friday		
12:30 - 1:00 Grooming	12:30 - 1:00 Grooming	12:30 - 1:00 Grooming	12:30 - 1:00 Grooming	12:30 - 1:00 Grooming		
1:00 - 1:30 Gross Motor Activity	1:00 - 1:30 Fine Motor Craft	1:00 - 1:30 Gross Motor Activity	1:00 - 1:30 Fine Motor Craft	1:00 - 1:30 Rec/Leisure Activity		
1:30 - 2:15 Unit Activity	1:30 - 2:15 Unit Activity	1:30 - 2:15 Unit Activity	1:30 - 2:15 Unit Activity	1:30 - 2:15 Unit Activity		
2:15 - 2:30 Recess	2:15 - 2:30 Recess	2:15 - 2:30 Recess	2:15 - 2:30 Recess	2:15 - 2:30 Recess		
2:30 - 3:00 Snack Time	2:30 - 3:00 Snack Time	2:30 - 3:00 Snack Time	2:30 - 3:00 Snack Time	2:30 - 3:00 Snack Time		

Level: Elementary

Domain: **Literacy**

Curriculum Goals:

Students will participate in classroom instructional activities:

- ❑ remain seated demonstrating visual and/or auditory attention to the lesson
- ❑ recognize own name and names of other students
- ❑ recognize date, current month, weather-related words, and menu items
- ❑ respond to questions, make comments, complete open-ended sentences
- ❑ follow one and two step directions during classroom activities
- ❑ complete center activities by interacting with an adult supervisor
- ❑ complete given seat work with minimal teacher prompts

Students will demonstrate language skills:

- ❑ identify objects and related actions
- ❑ identify words by category
- ❑ identify words by function
- ❑ associate describing words with nouns/objects

Students will demonstrate reading skills:

- ❑ recognize letters within words
- ❑ identify initial letters and sounds of words
- ❑ apply decoding skills to recognize unknown words
- ❑ recognize given sight words from unit topics
- ❑ recognize given basic sight words
- ❑ retell stories

❏ read simple sentences

❏ associate objects and actions to picture representations and text

Students will demonstrate writing skills:

❏ develop fine motor skills for coloring and cutting

❏ write own name from memory

❏ form letters to write/copy words

❏ write/spell given words from memory

❏ type words on the computer

❏ combine words to write/type simple sentences

❏ make computer selections to produce sentences and stories

Students will recognize vocabulary related to various unit topics:

❏ school: school activities, names of teachers, students, school rules

❏ personal ID: parents, siblings

❏ seasonal: Fall, weather, activities, clothing

❏ holidays: Thanksgiving, Christmas, Chanukah

❏ grooming: daily routines

❏ job awareness: librarian, grocery clerk, nurse, restaurant helper

❏ community: forms of transportation

❏ nature: forest animal names, homes

❏ clothing: items, activities, weather

❏ home: jobs to help

Students will demonstrate number skills:

- ❏ recognize numbers 1-30

- ❏ count objects in daily activities

- ❏ copy/type numbers

- ❏ understand pre-addition and subtraction concepts

- ❏ understand + and - symbols to complete problems to 10

Students will demonstrate money skills:

- ❏ recognize coins and match to cards

- ❏ recognize dollar amounts in a price tag under $10 and count dollar bills

- ❏ recognize value of one dollar, penny, nickel, dime, quarter

Students will demonstrate time skills:

- ❏ identify special activities, holidays, and birthdays on a calendar

- ❏ recognize and match time equations (0:00) to activities in schedule

- ❏ tell time to the hour on regular and digital clocks

- ❏ recognize days of the week and the sequence of days

- ❏ identify current month

Students will use measurement tools:

- ❏ use measuring cups for cooking

Domain: **Communication**

Curriculum Goals:

Students' present modes of communication will be expanded to increase effective interaction and vocabulary. Use of multi-modes will be encouraged. Students with alternate communication needs will be assessed for appropriate devices:

❑ eye gaze/visual attention

❑ switch activation of device

❑ scanning, with or without auditory cueing

❑ manual signs for functional information

❑ communication device for personal use

❑ picture symbol books/boards

❑ verbal

Students will demonstrate use of effective communication functions:

❑ convey basic needs and wants

❑ initiate greetings and respond to social greeting rituals

❑ respond to questions and relay information

❑ make requests and ask questions

❑ interact with peers in turn taking situations

❑ make appropriate comments during activities

Students will increase use of a personal communication book as an alternative means to clarify responses and to encourage verbalizations:

❑ utilize pages for personal information and activities

❑ utilize pages for interactions and vocabulary during units

Level: Elementary

Domain: **Participation with Typical Peers**

Curriculum Goals:

Students will develop appropriate social skills with second or third grade students in the regular classroom, at recess, and at lunch. Students will remain with the classmates and grade level that is appropriately designed for their age:

❑ integrate communication to greet and interact with peers

Students will develop group participation with second or third grade students in the regular classroom:

❑ sit with the group during an activity

❑ indicate appropriate means to gain attention from teacher for a response

❑ follow directions expected of other students with or without prompting

Students will develop skills in appropriate areas of second or third grade:

❑ respond to appropriate questions during a group activity

❑ share equipment at recess with or without adult intervention

❑ eat lunch in the cafeteria with minimal adult intervention

❑ participate in Art, Physical Education, and/or Music with or without adult assistance

Domain: **Independent Living**

Curriculum Goals:

Students will develop self-help skills into daily life:

- ❑ indicate need, assist in, and/or care for self when restrooming

- ❑ use appropriate utensils during lunch and snack periods

- ❑ perform daily grooming routines with minimal prompts

- ❑ remove and put on own clothing items, or assist as much as possible

- ❑ mobile students will independently move around the classroom, school

- ❑ non-ambulatory students will have appropriate equipment to move around

- ❑ develop gross motor skills for mobility/access to classroom, equipment

- ❑ state personal ID information of name, address, and family members

Students will participate in home help activities:

- ❑ locate items, follow simple recipe directions to complete cooking activity

- ❑ demonstrate table setting skills

- ❑ assist in table clearing and cooking cleanup

- ❑ sort and fold simple clothing items and towels

- ❑ pick up toys

Level: Elementary

Domain: **Community**

Curriculum Goals:

Students will develop an awareness of their community and places in it:

❑ identify community locations and things they might do there

❑ identify their address

❑ identify modes of transportation that can be used to travel to different places

Students will identify people who help us in the community. Students will recognize jobs performed by these people:

❑ librarian

❑ doctor

❑ grocery store clerk

❑ restaurant worker

❑ firefighter, police officer, letter carrier

Students will demonstrate pedestrian safety when walking to and around the community.

Domain: **Recreation/Leisure**

Curriculum Goals:

Students will participate in age appropriate recreation/leisure activities:

- ❏ perform gross motor tasks for walking, running, ball playing, etc.

- ❏ perform physical therapy activities under direction of physical therapist

- ❏ demonstrate turn taking in group circle games

- ❏ learn and participate in a variety of board games

- ❏ learn and follow rules of the playground during recess

- ❏ demonstrate appropriate use of toys during free play activities

- ❏ explore independent play activities, including coloring, puzzles, books

- ❏ pick up toys when directed to do so

- ❏ participate in role-playing activities

- ❏ demonstrate appropriate interactions and turn taking with peers

Level: Elementary

Domain: **Vocational**

Curriculum Goals:

Students will be able to complete given activities in the classroom:

- ❑ follow one and two step directions

- ❑ remain on task to complete an activity with minimal prompting

- ❑ show a willingness to try new activities

- ❑ request assistance as needed

- ❑ work cooperatively with other students

Students will complete classroom jobs:

- ❑ perform routine tasks, such as calendar and weather helper

- ❑ set up and clean up snack table

Students will care for their own belongings:

- ❑ place and locate coat and book bag in coat rack; place papers in book bag

- ❑ locate and use grooming equipment with assistance, if needed

- ❑ get and return cafeteria tray at lunch time with or without assistance

- ❑ get out and return school materials for an activity

Name _____

Date _____

Circle Time Activities

Recognizes names of students:

❑ own

❑ classmates

❑ auditorily   ❑ manual sign   ❑ picture representation   ❑ written

Conveys events from home:

❑ verbally   ❑ using communication book/board

❑ recorded messages   ❑ communication device

Greetings:

❑ looks at the person greeting

❑ gives an appropriate greeting

❑ smiles   ❑ waves   ❑ verbal   ❑ voice device

❑ consistently responds to greetings

Attendance:

❑ counts boys/girls

❑ identifies number

❑ adds number of boys and girls

Calendar information:

identifies: ❑ day   ❑ yesterday   ❑ month

Weather information:

❑ identifies weather of the day

Menu:

❑ identifies food items on the daily menu

Attending behaviors:

❑ shows an awareness of circle time activities

❑ participates in activities

Circle Time: Activity Ideas

Morning Greetings

The morning circle time provides a structured way to learn social rituals and interactions that are appropriate in greetings. In this activity, students should be encouraged to initiate the interaction with another student of their choice, and make a greeting that gains the attention of the other person. The receiving student also needs to realize that it is important to respond to these greetings, even if in a nonverbal mode, i.e. a smile, a wave, or eye contact. This type of activity should be fast moving with a decreasing amount of prompts to facilitate greeting initiations and responses.

The greeting time is also an opportunity to find a means to continue the conversation with comments, such as "What have you been up to?" or "What did you do last night?" Students may respond with their own personal activities. The other student should then make a comment to the response, such as "That's cool" or "Sounds like fun." The Conversation Starter Overlay, page 24, is included which may be customized for each student or used as a classroom initiator.

Daily Attendance

This activity provides a means to incorporate meaningful addition concepts on a routine basis. One student may be selected as the leader thus requiring him/her to ask other students, "How many boys/girls are here?" This procedure may also be reversed to incorporate subtraction concepts. Use the Who Is Here? math addition activity, page 25, and the Attendance Chart Numbers cards, page 26, to determine how many students are in the class and how many are absent.

Calendar and Weather

Calendar time develops into an awareness of the present day/month and activities related to that day. Use a larger calendar to display these dates and special activities. The numbers on the calendar are daily reinforcement of number concepts to 30/31. Special holidays should be predicted ahead on the calendar. Again, this is an opportunity to designate one student as the leader so they must ask the questions of other students. Comments about the weather may be introduced at this time, i.e. "Yuck, I hate rainy days." Talking about the weather is a typical conversation starter used by adults. Related worksheets are included on pages 27-34.

Today's Menu

Menu Items Overlays I and II, pages 36 and 37, are included for typical school lunch menus. Students should identify the food items on the daily menu using the What's For Lunch Today? worksheet, page 35. They may make comments about what they like and don't like. They may also identify if they are eating the school lunch or have packed their lunch. This might be a good opportunity to "take a lunch count," having students pay as appropriate.

Level: Elementary

Daily Report

A daily report of the date, weather, and activities may be completed as an independent seat work activity or a center activity with adult assistance. This type of activity may have many variations of skills. Different students may write words, match words, or add picture symbols from the Daily Report Overlay, page 39, to complete this page. The format remains the same each day, however the information will change. It is a follow-up of the morning circle time information and provides a page that can be shared at home. (Encourage parents to use this page as a conversation starter with their child about the day at school.)

Communication

The information used in circle time can be readily programmed into a student's communication system. Since it is repeated daily it will get lots of use. However, this information can be rather boring if it is only used to respond to questions asked by an adult during a twenty minute period each day. Therefore, the use of this information should be incorporated into a variety of conversation starters and application situations. The use of questions and comments become critical elements. Adults who are facilitating the use of this vocabulary should strive to use it in a turn taking conversational direction.

Conversation Starter Overlay

Typical activities may be added to the blank spaces.

Level: Elementary

Who Is Here?

Count the boys and/or girls who are in class today.

boys

girls

+ _____

Attendance Chart Numbers

1	2	3	4
5	6	7	8
9	10	1	2
3	4	5	6
7	8	9	10

Level: Elementary

What Day Is Today?

Attach the appropriate picture symbol from page 29 below.

What Day Was Yesterday?

Attach the appropriate picture symbol from page 29 below.

Level: Elementary

Days Overlay

today

yesterday

Sunday

Monday

Tuesday

Wednesday

Thursday

Friday

What Month Is This?

Attach appropriate picture symbol from page 31 or 32 below.

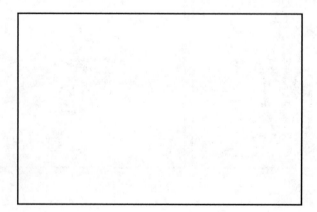

Level: Elementary

Months Overlay I

Months Overlay II

What Does The Weatherman Say Today?

Attach the appropriate picture symbols from page 34 below.

Weather Words Overlay

weather 	hot 	cold 
sunny 	rainy 	cool 
snowy 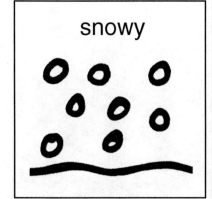	cloudy 	warm 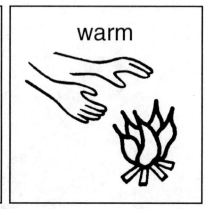

Level: Elementary

What's For Lunch Today?

Attach appropriate picture symbols from pages 36 and 37 below.

Menu Items Overlay I

pizza	hot dog	hamburger	sloppy joe
chicken sandwich	spaghetti	fish sandwich	ham sandwich
taco	chips	french fries	tater tot
mashed potatoes	peanut butter	butter bread	beans
carrot	salad	cheese	turkey

Level: Elementary

Menu Items Overlay II

cake	cookies	apple crisp	applesauce
fruit cocktail	peach	pear	pineapple
ice cream	pudding	corn	peas
chicken nuggets	grilled cheese	cheeseburger	chicken
milk	orange	banana	apple

Daily Report

Today is _____.

The weather is _____

and _____.

Special things we do today:

Attach picture symbols from page 39 below.

Name_____

_____

Level: Elementary

Daily Report Overlay

art class 	gym class 	music class 
speech therapy 	occupational therapy 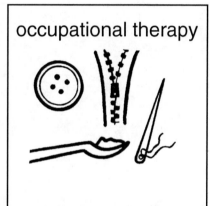	physical therapy 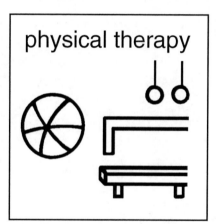
field trip 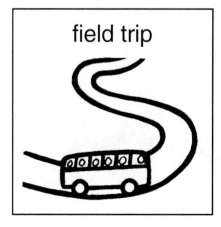	special program 	

Name _____

Date _____

Unit Topic: School Is Cool

Literacy:

- ❑ demonstrates listening and attending behaviors during story reading
- ❑ participates in the story
- ❑ recognizes the school/class rules
- ❑ recognizes school supplies and use:
  - ❑ pencil   ❑ crayon   ❑ glue   ❑ book   ❑ scissors
- ❑ recognizes school activities
- ❑ recognizes basic sight words
- ❑ recognizes unit topic sight words
- ❑ recognizes initial letters/sounds in words
- ❑ copies/writes/types unit words
- ❑ has developed fine motor skills for coloring, cutting, and pasting
- ❑ counts objects/identifies number
- ❑ has been introduced to basic addition concepts

Communication:

- ❑ communicates during activities by _____
- ❑ responds to questions related to topic activities
- ❑ makes requests for needed materials
- ❑ uses "please" and "thank you"

Independent/Community Living:

- ❑ moves around the school to participate in activities
- ❑ follows the school/class rules

Recreation/Leisure:

- ❑ plays appropriately on recess equipment
- ❑ participates in independent leisure activities, i.e. coloring, looking at books

Vocational:

- ❑ follows simple directions in classroom activities
- ❑ completes assignments with minimal prompts

Level: Elementary   41

School Rules

school

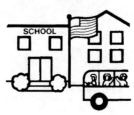

Dear Parents:

As the school year begins, we will be learning the rules of the school in our first unit. The rules create an expectancy of behaviors for the classroom, the school building, and life in general. These rules are as follows:

- *Listen to the teacher.*
- *Walk in the hallways around school.*
- *Keep your hands to yourself.*
- *Don't touch other people's things.*

This year we will put high emphasis on early learning reading skills. Vocabulary introduced during this unit are objects, actions, and activities that are encountered in the school day.

Sincerely,

Level: Elementary

The Story: School Is Cool

This story, pages 45-57, introduces the rules that are generally important for school. As students travel the halls and attend regular education programs, it is increasingly important that they realize the rules that other students follow. Sometimes, other teachers in the school building need to be made aware that, yes, we do expect our children with special needs to learn the rules of the school ... and they may remind the student of these rules as they would "typical" children.

The story is a good opportunity to invite the school principal into the classroom. He may read the story to the students and discuss the rules of the school.

An additional worksheet is provided on page 61 to match the school rules.

Students with limited mobility or physical ability should also learn the rules. They may not be the aggressor, but they may need to learn a way to express to others "Don't touch my things."

Suggested Vocabulary for Reading Activities

Vocabulary Cards (symbols/words) are included, pages 59 and 60, with the suggested vocabulary. These vocabulary words include school actions, school supplies, and special classes. They may be incorporated into picture symbol recognition, sight word activities, phonics instruction, etc. You may want to introduce only a limited number of words per week. Some students may use these words for spelling lists. The way these words are utilized with each student may vary greatly according to his/her ability and skill levels. Be creative in the use of vocabulary. Customize the presentation of the words specific to a student's abilities/disabilities.

Use the suggestions in the Reading/Spelling Activities section, page 5, to create reading and spelling games with the words for this unit.

Basic sight words during this unit may include "I can" which is used in several carrier phrases.

Mini-Story

The mini-story, pages 62-64, reinforces the rules. Take photographs of the students doing various activities at school or have the students draw their own picture. Arrange the pages into booklet form to read.

Math Activities

The worksheets included, pages 65 and 66, are starter activities for counting and addition activities. Creating real-life situations using the students' school supplies will provide further opportunities to count and add.

Students with limited physical abilities should be encouraged to participate in all literacy activities using alternate modes of expression.

Arts and Crafts

An Art Activities Overlay, page 67, is included that can be utilized for arts and crafts projects. Besides developing fine motor skills, these types of projects offer an opportunity for students to make requests for needed supplies. Rather than the students getting the supplies beforehand, the teacher may keep them thus requiring the students to ask for what they need. Daily center activities need not be elaborate. A shapes activity, pages 68 and 69, is included that can be created using crayons, scissors, and glue. Similar activities, such as the Matching worksheets, pages 70 and 71, may be created to provide this opportunity to follow directions and make requests for needed supplies.

School Tours

Tour the school and locate the rooms where students will attend Art, Music, and Physical Education. Use the Vocabulary Cards (symbols/words), pages 59 and 60, to mark these rooms. Assist students in getting to these locations during designated times. However, begin to put greater responsibility on the students to find their own way to the particular classroom, or get a buddy from the classroom to stop by and walk with the student to class.

Remember, students should be encouraged to attend regular education classes with age and grade appropriate peers. When an entire "special class" attends a class, they tend to remain isolated in a group with the other special students. If one or two students attend with the typically developing classroom, they are more likely to become a part of the regular class, even with a buddy to assist them.

Computer Activities

Create an enlarged keyboard using the rules on the School Is Cool Overlay, page 58. Program this overlay to type the rules. Students will select a colored paper to type and print the school rules on. Hang these rules around the hallways of the school for reminders to all students.

Additional Activity Sources

Quick Tech Readable, Repeatable Stories and Activities, "Where's My Book?" Mayer-Johnson Co.

Units, "Alphabet," Mayer-Johnson Co.

Rules for School

Listen

Walk

Don't Touch

School Is Cool

Rules for School

Listen

Walk

Don't Touch

We're back to school.
Mr. B. is putting up the rules.

school   Mr. B.   Rules

Level: Elementary

"Remember," says Mr. B.,
"school is cool when you follow the rules."

Jason goes to his classroom.
His teacher is talking.
Jason is talking too.

teacher talk Jason talk

Level: Elementary

 Listen to your teacher.

Here is Mr. B.
He shows Jason the rules.
"Listen to your teacher."

Rules   Mr. B.   listen   teacher

Time for recess.
Jason pushes a boy.
Jason hits a girl.

recess

hit

Level: Elementary

Keep your hands
to yourself.

Here is Mr. B.
He shows Jason the rules.
"Keep your hands to yourself."

Mr. B. Rules hit

Time for lunch.
Jason takes a boy's cookie.
He takes a girl's milk.

lunch cookie milk

 Don't touch other people's things.

Here is Mr. B.
He shows Jason the rules.
"Don't touch other people's things."

Mr. B. | Rules | Don't touch

Time for Art class.
Jason runs down the hall.
He runs into Art class.

Art class   run

Walk in the halls.

Here is Mr. B.
He shows Jason the rules.
"Walk in the halls."

Mr. B.

Rules

walk

Time for the bus to go home.
Mom is waiting.
"Did you have a good day at school?"

bus　　Mom　　day

Rules for School

"Guess what?" says Jason.
"School is cool now that I know the rules."

school   cool

School Is Cool Overlay

School is cool. 	Know the rules. 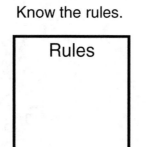	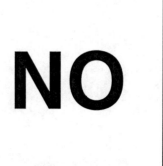
listen 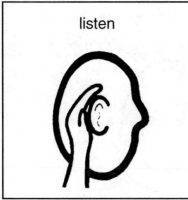	walk 	Don't touch other's things. 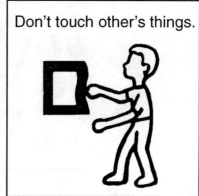
Keep hands to yourself. 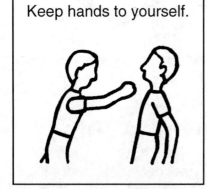	I know the rules. 	Sorry, I forgot the rules. 

Level: Elementary

Vocabulary Cards (symbols)

walk	listen	eat	play
read	color	cut	write
pencil	crayon	glue	scissors
book	Art	Music	P.E.
recess	lunch		

Vocabulary Cards (words)

walk	listen	eat	play
read	color	cut	write
pencil	crayon	glue	scissors
book	Art	Music	Physical Education
recess	lunch		

Level: Elementary

Matching

Match the rules.

listen

Don't hit

walk

Don't touch

Don't touch

listen

Don't hit

walk

School Is Cool

with _____

I can listen to
my teacher.

Level: Elementary

I can play at recess.

I can walk to my class.

I can eat lunch.

School is cool.
I know the rules.

listen

walk

Keep your hands to yourself.

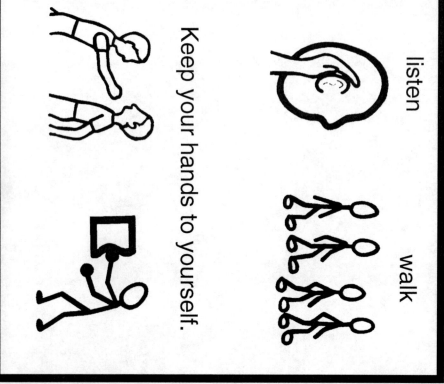

Level: Elementary

Counting

Count the school supplies.

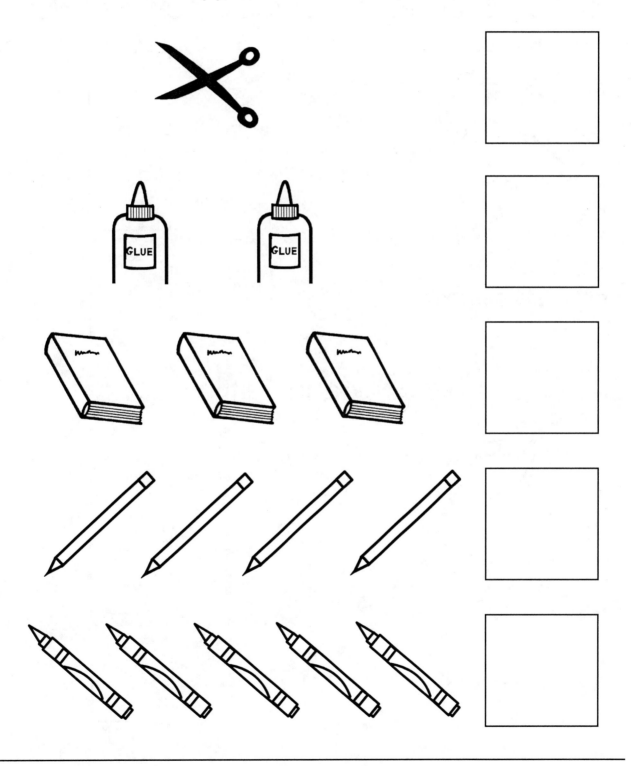

Addition Skills

Bob has 2 red pencils and 3 yellow pencils.

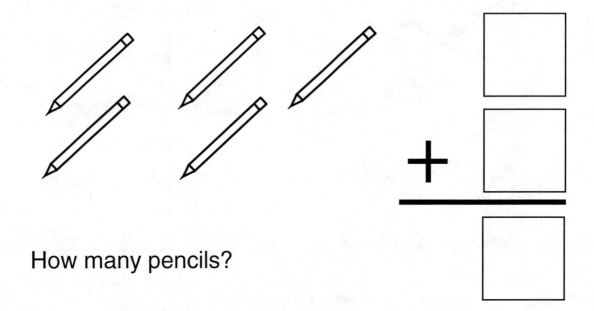

How many pencils?

Sara has 1 big book and 3 little books.

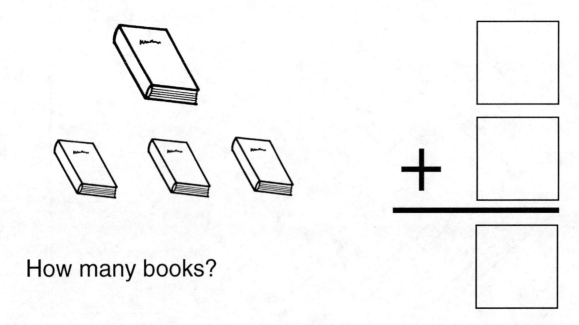

How many books?

Level: Elementary

Art Activities Overlay

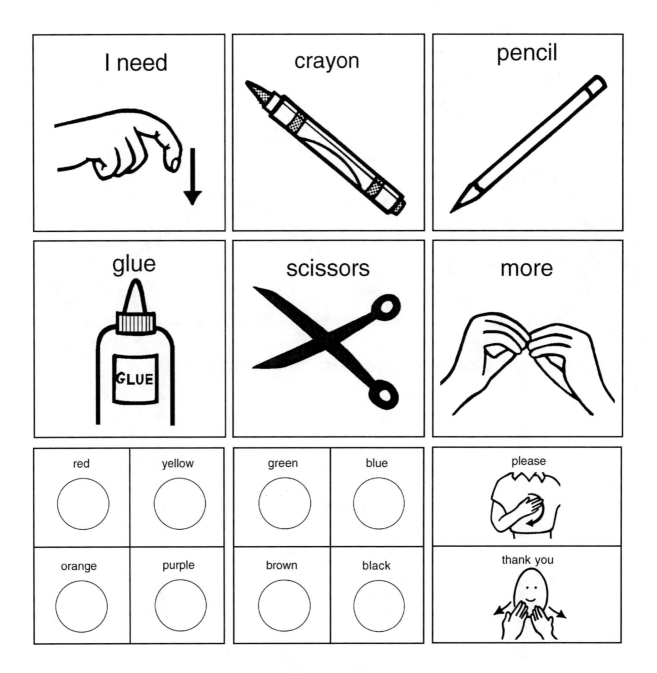

I need

crayon

pencil

glue

scissors

more

| red | yellow | green | blue | please |
| orange | purple | brown | black | thank you |

Shapes Activity

Color the circle yellow.
Color the triangle brown.
Color the square red.
Cut out the shapes.
Glue them on page 69.

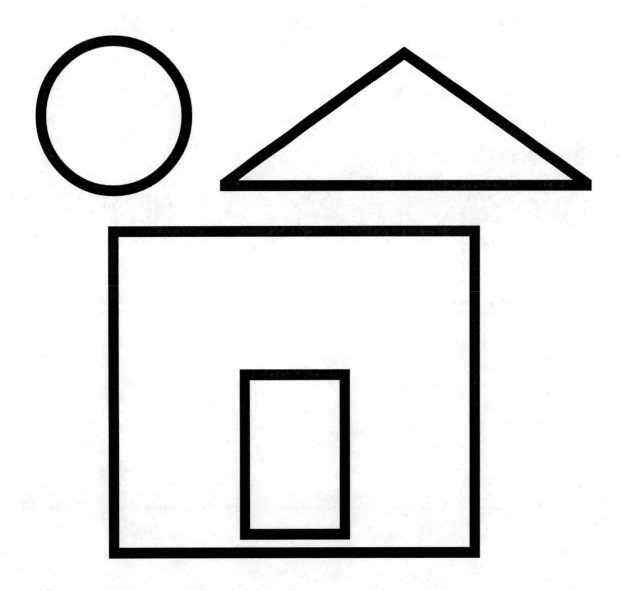

Level: Elementary

Shapes Activity

Matching

Match the word to the picture symbol.

book   crayon   glue
   scissors   pencil

Level: Elementary

Matching

Match the action to the picture symbol.

I can read.

I can cut.

I can color.

I can glue.

I can write.

Name _____

Date _____

Unit Topic: Fall Fantasy

Literacy:
- ❑ demonstrates listening and attending behaviors during story reading
- ❑ participates in the story
- ❑ recognizes Fall as a changing season
- ❑ recognizes descriptive words
- ❑ identifies color words
- ❑ identifies basic sight words
- ❑ identifies unit topic sight words
- ❑ recognizes initial letters/sounds in words
- ❑ copies/writes/types unit words
- ❑ recognizes weather temperatures of Fall
- ❑ counts by 10's

Communication:
- ❑ communicates during activities by _____
- ❑ asks questions to gain information
- ❑ responds to questions related to topic activities
- ❑ uses descriptive words
- ❑ uses appropriate means to express feelings

Independent/Community Living:
- ❑ recognizes changes in nature
- ❑ identifies appropriate clothing to wear on chilly days
- ❑ identifies feelings
- ❑ participates in outdoor cleanup activities
- ❑ participates in simple cooking activities

Recreation/Leisure:
- ❑ participates in outdoor seasonal activities
- ❑ participates in seasonal activities

Vocational:
- ❑ follows simple directions in classroom activities
- ❑ completes assignments with minimal prompts

Level: Elementary   73

Fall Fantasy

Fall

Dear Parents:

This month's topic explores the changes that occur in the Fall season. Besides the changes in nature, there are changes in the weather and the clothing that we wear on the cooler days. In our reading activities, we will learn the color words and use of describing words.

Special activities related to Halloween will occur this month. We will explore various feelings as we decorate our pumpkin faces. This will introduce ways that we too can express these feelings.

Sincerely,

Level: Elementary

The Story: Fall Is On The Way

This story, pages 77-86, incorporates colors in the changing season of Fall and the holiday of Halloween. Using these seasonal concepts, descriptive words are introduced. Fall also is a transitional period for the weather. With these changes in temperature comes the need to wear heavier clothing for the chilly days.

There is a repetitive line in this story that can be incorporated for single switch users with a tape recorder and switch.

Suggested Vocabulary for Reading Activities

The Vocabulary Cards (symbols/words), pages 88 and 89, include words associated with the Fall season, colors, and basic feelings. The color words may be combined with several objects on the vocabulary cards for different meaning (e.g., red apple, green apple, yellow apple).

Use the suggestions in the Reading/Spelling Activities section, page 5, to create reading and spelling games with the words for this unit.

The Complete The Sentence worksheet, page 90, is included for combining words using descriptors. Other sentences may be created using symbol or word cards in the format of: "The _____ is _____ and _____." This will facilitate the use of the basic sight words of "the," "is," and "and."

Color Book

Each student should have the opportunity to create the Fall Color Book, pages 91-95. Pictures in the book may be colored or painted. The sentence at the bottom of each page should be read to determine what color to make the object. Use the Art Activities Overlay, page 67, to encourage the students to request certain colors when doing these pages.

Associated activities may be done when completing a page in the book. Examples might include:
- Pumpkin: Cut out a jack-o'-lantern or paint faces on a pumpkin.
- Apples: Make applesauce using the recipe on page 96.
- Leaves: Make leaf prints, laying the leaf under a piece of paper and coloring on the paper with the side of a crayon.
- Mask: Make a Halloween mask out of a paper sack.

Math Activities

Using the thermometer on page 97, count by tens to 90. Discuss the temperatures and meanings between hot, warm, chilly, and cold. Create a classroom thermometer using the worksheet with a piece of elastic from top to bottom. Color a section of the elastic red to mark the daily temperature. Each day when the temperature is marked, discuss the types of clothing that are appropriate for the day.

Nature Trips

Explore the outdoor nature opportunities in your locality. Several suggestions might include:

- A walk through the woods/park. Take note of the changes related to Fall. Discuss clothing that should be worn on this trip using the Fall Clothing worksheet, page 98. Make a list of "scavenger items" to locate on the trip (e.g., a red leaf, nut, flower, etc.)
- Visit a pumpkin patch. Some farms will have tours through a pumpkin patch. Allow the students to select their own pumpkin. Discuss the sizes of the pumpkins — small, medium, and large.
- Take a ride on a hay wagon. Sing songs along the way.

Clean Up the Neighborhood

Plan an activity to rake leaves and/or clean up litter. This might be done at a student's home or a neighbor's home near the school. Encourage each student to participate in completing this activity, either by raking and/or putting leaves and trash into a bag.

Feelings Faces

Use the pumpkin faces on page 99 to introduce feelings. We can recognize feelings by facial expressions. Discuss things that make us feel this way. Examples might include:

- Happy: When we get candy for Halloween.
- Mad: If someone takes our candy.
- Sad: If we lose our candy.
- Scared: When a spooky Halloween character comes to our house.

Presenting unit activities on feelings allows for a nonconfrontational situation when feelings can be defined. Pumpkins are often carved or painted to express different feelings. During a classroom carving activity, ask the students to select a feeling to put on their pumpkin.

Having various feelings is normal and healthy. However, students with limited verbal ability may develop less than appropriate ways to express these feelings. If a student is using a communication device, plan for appropriate messages to express different feelings. Facilitate use of these messages by modeling in specific situations when these feelings are present for the child.

Additional Activity Sources

Interactive Augmentative Communication Program, "Halloween," Mayer-Johnson Co.

More Hands-on Reading, "Big Pumpkin," Mayer-Johnson Co.

I Can Cook, Too!, "October Themes," page 49, Mayer-Johnson Co.

Storytime, Holiday Fun!, "Stirring the Brew," page 38, Creative Communicating.

Fall Is On The Way

This chilly, chilly day
tells me Fall is on the way.

chilly 　　day 　　Fall

Look at the leaves,
changing colors.
Look at the leaves,
falling down.

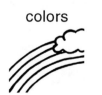
colors

leaves

fall

And this chilly, chilly day
tells me Fall is on the way.

chilly   day   Fall

Level: Elementary

Look at the pumpkin,
big and orange.
Look at the pumpkin
with a bright happy face.

big

pumpkin

orange

happy

And this chilly, chilly day
tells me Fall is on the way.

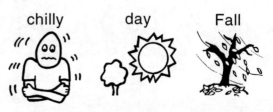

chilly   day   Fall

Level: Elementary

Look at the apples,
up in the tree.
Look at the apples,
shiny and red.

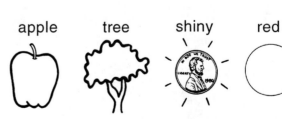

apple   tree   shiny   red

And this chilly, chilly day
tells me Fall is on the way.

chilly   day   Fall

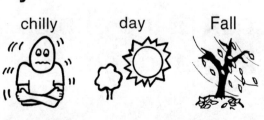

Level: Elementary

Look at the masks
for Halloween.
Look at the masks,
some scary, some funny.

masks

Halloween

scary

funny

Leaves and apples and pumpkins,
and this chilly, chilly day.
All this tells me Fall is on the way.

leaves	apple	pumpkin	chilly	day	Fall

Level: Elementary

Fall Is On The Way Overlay

Fall	look	chilly
leaves	pumpkin	apple
masks		What do you see?

Vocabulary Cards (symbols)

pumpkin	apple	leaf	tree
Fall	Halloween	cold	cat
happy	scared	mad	sad
red	yellow	orange	green
black	brown	blue	purple

Level: Elementary

Vocabulary Cards (words)

pumpkin	apple	leaf	tree
Fall	Halloween	cold	cat
happy	scared	mad	sad
red	yellow	orange	green
black	brown	blue	purple

Complete The Sentence

Cut out the picture symbols at the bottom of the page.
Glue them in the appropriate box to complete the sentence.

The ☐ is **shiny** and red.

The ☐ is **soft** and black.

The ☐ is **big** and green.

The ☐ is **hard** and orange.

cat   pumpkin   apple   tree

Level: Elementary

The pumpkin
is orange.

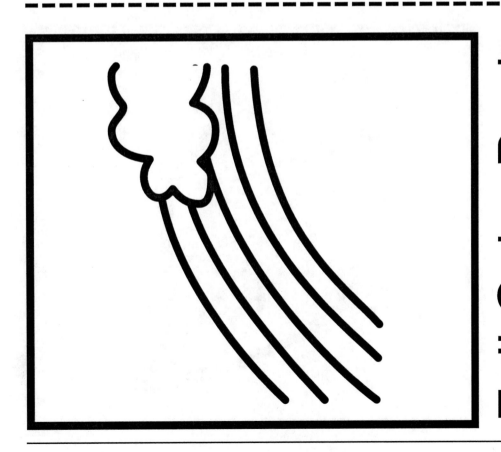

Fall Color Book
by _____

The tree is green.

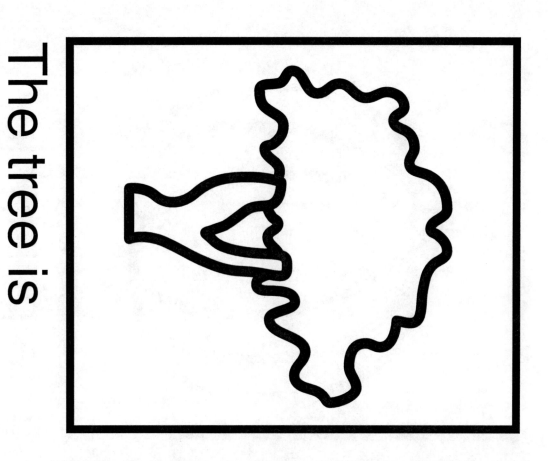

The leaf is yellow.

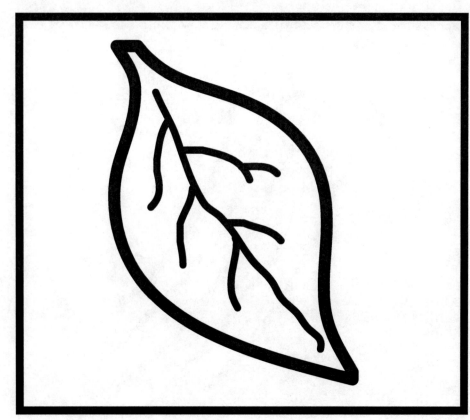

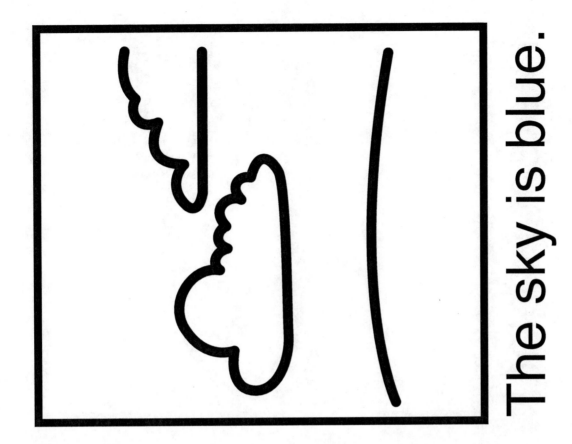

The sky is blue.

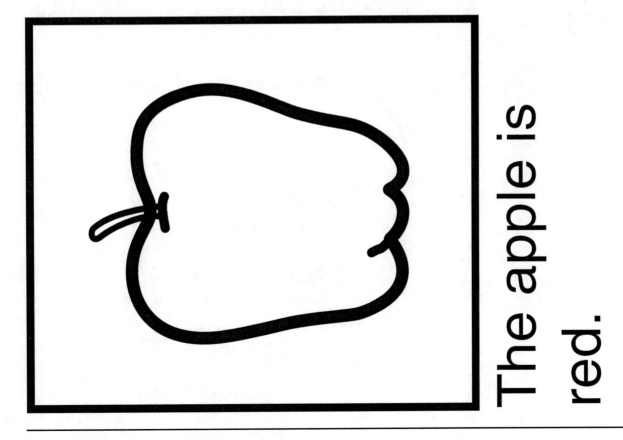

The apple is red.

The cat is black.

The mask is purple.

Level: Elementary

This is my
favorite color.

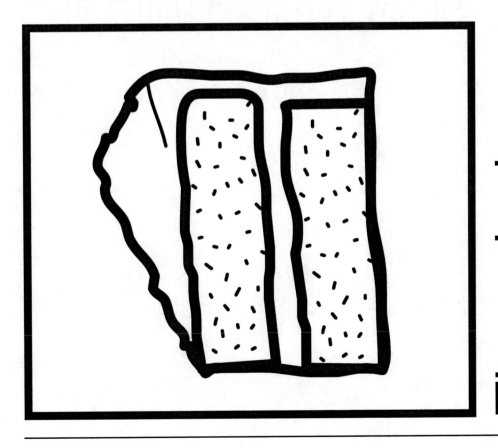

The cake is
brown.

Applesauce

 Cut apples into slices.

 Cook in a pan.

 Strain in a food mill.

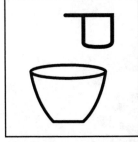 Add sugar.

 Stir!

Level: Elementary

Thermometer

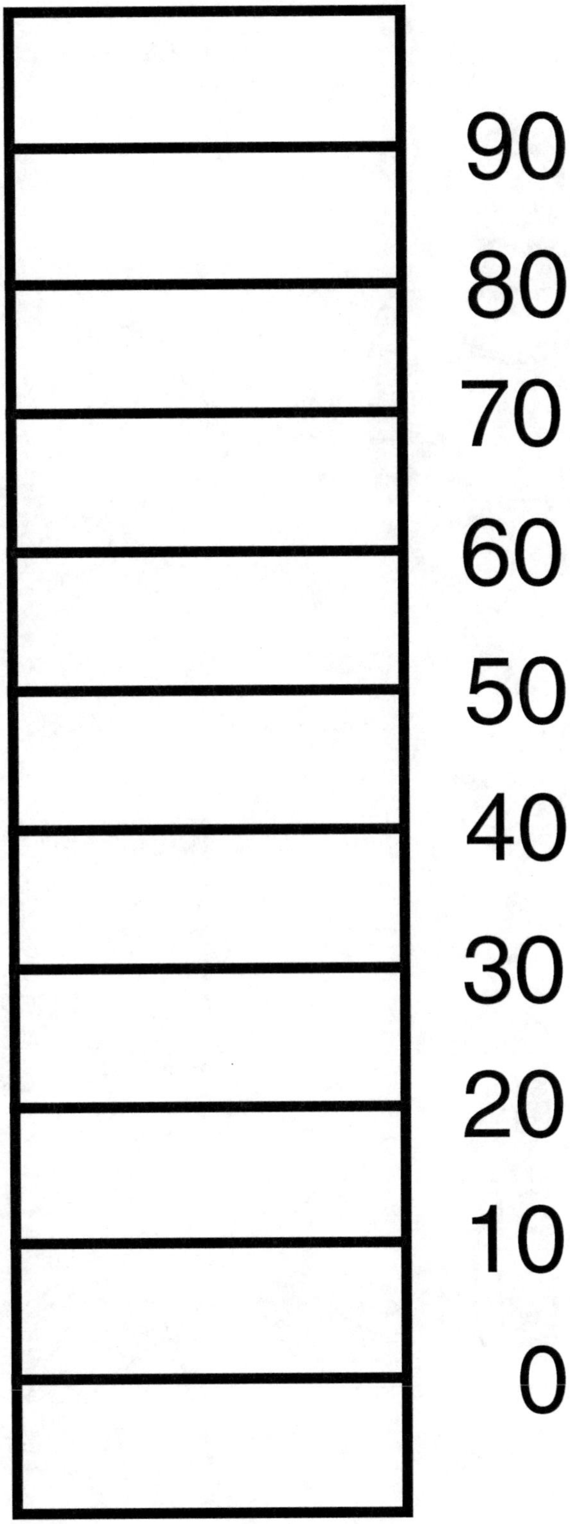

90

80

70

60   warm

50

40   chilly

30

20

10

0

hot

cold

Fall Clothing

Circle the clothes you might wear on a chilly Fall day.

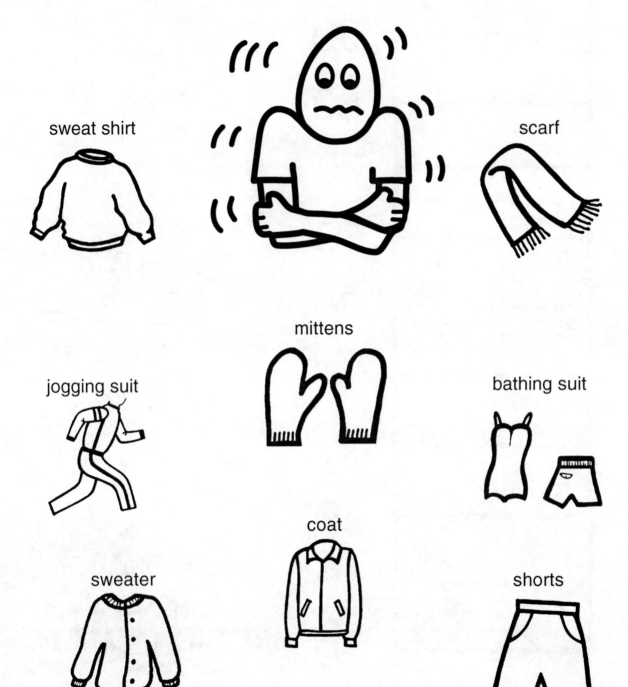

sweat shirt

scarf

mittens

jogging suit

bathing suit

coat

sweater

shorts

Level: Elementary

Feelings Faces

happy

mad

sad

scared

Name _____

Date _____

Unit Topic: Thanksgiving Dinner

Literacy:
- ❑ demonstrates listening and attending behaviors during story reading
- ❑ participates in the story
- ❑ recognizes food items for Thanksgiving dinner
- ❑ identifies Thanksgiving as a holiday
- ❑ makes associations between things that "go together"
- ❑ recognizes basic sight words
- ❑ recognizes unit topic sight words
- ❑ applies decoding skills to words
- ❑ matches coins for amounts up to $1.00
- ❑ recognizes prices of objects to $5.00
- ❑ locates numbers
    - ❑ calculator   ❑ microwave

Communication:
- ❑ communicates during activities by _____
- ❑ responds to questions related to unit topic
- ❑ asks questions to gain information
- ❑ responds to social interactions

Independent Living:
- ❑ participates in mealtime activities
    - ❑ sets table   ❑ clears table after meal   ❑ participates in food preparation
- ❑ recognizes foods in food group categories
- ❑ uses a microwave for cooking

Community Living:
- ❑ identifies the grocery store as a place to purchase food
- ❑ participates in grocery shopping
- ❑ uses money to make purchases in a grocery store

Recreation/Leisure:
- ❑ demonstrates turn taking in game playing activities

Vocational:
- ❑ follows simple directions to complete a task
- ❑ works cooperatively in group activities

Thanksgiving

turkey

Dear Parents:

This month's unit is about preparing a Thanksgiving dinner. We will cover many skills, including food preparation, food prices, and identifying foods in the food group categories. We will practice our math skills by using the microwave and the calculator. The story with this unit matches foods that "go together."

At the end of the unit, we will prepare our own Thanksgiving feast.

Sincerely,

Level: Elementary

The Story: Get It Together

This story, pages 106-115, is based around preparing food for a Thanksgiving meal, with many of the typical foods associated with this meal. The foods are grouped as they "go together," such as mashed potatoes and gravy, peas and carrots, etc. This story is also a means to introduce the food groups.

The story serves as a springboard for various cooking activities. Emphasis is also placed on the prices of these food items and purchasing them in the grocery story.

Suggested Vocabulary for Reading Activities

The Vocabulary Cards (symbols/words), pages 117 and 118, in this unit are food words and the food group categories. Grocery store flyers are an excellent source to obtain additional pictures of these foods for matching activities. Shopping lists may be made using the symbols or words from this unit.

The word "and" is incorporated in worksheets and activities that combine two foods that go together. This can be incorporated in a variety of reading activities with carrier phrases, such as "I like..."

Use the suggestions in the Reading/Spelling Activities section, page 5, to create reading and spelling games with the words for this unit.

Things That Go Together

Besides the foods in this unit that go together, there are several objects that can be matched and sorted as "together" things. Create a center basket with objects that might be matched. Worksheets are included, pages 119-121, for written forms of connecting "together words." These could be laminated. Attach a piece of yarn to each symbol with a punched hole at the matching symbols. Students will complete the activity by "sewing" between the "together" items.

Money Skills

This unit emphasizes the money skills associated with prices of food. These types of activities may be incorporated at various levels depending on the student's individual ability.

- Match coins to determine a given amount. A worksheet is included, page 122, for coin matching. Students who can count amounts may be given the amount and asked to determine the coins without matching.

- Determine dollars and cents in a price over $1.00. These activities, pages 123 and 124, introduce the use of the "$" (dollar sign) and the "." (decimal point) used to mark dollar and cents amounts. Students should practice reading these amounts, first by covering half of the price and determining the dollar amount, then by covering the other half and reading the cents amount.

Money Skills (Cont.)

- Practice locating these numbers on a calculator. A large paper calculator is included, page 125, or a large key calculator may be used. Students will touch or locate the number and include the "." between the dollar and cents amounts. Students with limited physical ability should be encouraged to locate numbers in a scanning manner.

- Determine the amount of dollar bills for a purchase. When an amount is over $1.00, the students should determine the dollar amount and "add one more." (For example, $2.50 would be two dollar bills plus one more, or three.) This technique will enable students to have an effective means to determine the amount of money needed when making a purchase. It also limits the money that might be lost if they are in a situation where someone might take advantage of them; they can never lose more than $1.00 this way. In the early stages of going into the community to make purchases, students should not be expected to make large purchases, such as a $30.00 grocery bill. They should only be allowed to make small purchases, under $5.00. Therefore, they would carry with them only five one dollar bills. "Dollar bills" are included on a worksheet, page 126, which may be duplicated for play money to use in these money skill activities.

Grocery Shopping

Practice grocery shopping may be done in the classroom by making a shopping list and using empty containers or picture symbols for the grocery items. Prices should be included on the items. Students will practice locating and identifying the price on the items. This is also a good time to have the students keep their money in a fanny pack, wallet, or purse as they would if shopping in the store.

Grocery store flyers are another source of shopping activities. If the student has a list of items, he/she may look through the flyer for the needed items then determine the amount of money for making this purchase.

When traveling into the community for grocery shopping, it is advisable to make several small trips with one or two students going at a time. Large groups and large purchases do not lend themselves to the skills that are being reinforced in this unit. Again, when the students are going shopping they should be responsible for carrying the money for these purchases.

Communication in the Community

Shopping practice in the classroom should include those social interactions that are frequently encountered in the grocery store. Students need to realize that if someone greets them, they should respond. Students should have a means to express a response to these interactions, even if through a smile or eye contact. This is also a time to remind the students of safety rules when traveling in the community.

Students should also have a means to request assistance in the store. For example, "Where is the butter?" Communication aids should be programmed for these situations.

Store clerks will frequently look to the accompanying adult for clarification. If the student is equipped with a means to respond to the questions, he/she should be encouraged to do this. If you frequent these stores, the clerks will soon learn that the students can respond for themselves. Students with limited physical ability should also travel into the community and have a means to respond to the interactions they encounter.

Cooking Thanksgiving Dinner

This unit also offers the opportunity to prepare simple foods. A Thanksgiving feast may be prepared, inviting either parents or school friends.

The majority of the foods for this meal can be prepared in a microwave. Several recipes are included, pages 127-129, for canned turkey, instant potatoes, and canned gravy. Similar recipes could be included for the foods that you select. These recipes may be inserted into a clear page protector and kept in a ring binder for further use. Some of the recipes do not have the amount included. This way they can be customized for the number of people that you will be serving.

A large paper microwave is included, page 130, for practice on setting the time on a microwave. This could also be created on an enlarged keyboard.

When preparing food for a meal like this, keep in mind what sorts of practical application this student will use as an adult. It is likely that a pumpkin pie may never be made from scratch. Therefore, this might be an item that is purchased in the grocery store or ordered from a bakery.

Food Groups

A Food Wheel is included, page 131, that may be used in conjunction with the Food Guide Pyramid (USDA). Early skills of learning the food groups involves sorting by categories, with emphasis on planning meals that have something from every food group. This circle can be used to create activities involving sorting and meal planning. The school's daily lunch might also be sorted in this manner.

Additional Activity Sources

Units, "Cooking Corn," Mayer-Johnson Co.

Hands-on Reading, "Food Unit," Mayer-Johnson Co.

I Can Cook, Too!, "November Themes," Mayer-Johnson Co.

Interactive Augmentative Communication Program, "Food," Mayer-Johnson Co.

Storytime, Holiday Fun!, "The Big Dinner," Creative Communicating.

Get It Together

Let's get it together
for Thanksgiving dinner.

together Thanksgiving dinner

"I can help," said Heather.
"I can put it together."

help together

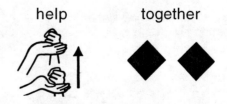

Level: Elementary

Turkey and dressing.
These go together.

turkey　　　dressing　　　together

Mashed potatoes and gravy.
These go together.

mashed potatoes   gravy   together

Peas and carrots.
These go together.

Rolls and butter.
These go together.

roll butter together

Pumpkin pie and whipped cream.
These go together.

pie   whipped cream   together

We've got it together
for Thanksgiving dinner.

together   Thanksgiving   dinner

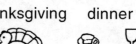

Let's eat!

Get It Together Overlay

These go together.	turkey	dressing
mashed potatoes	gravy	peas
carrot	roll	butter

Level: Elementary

Vocabulary Cards (symbols)

turkey	dressing	mashed potatoe	gravy
peas	carrot	roll	butter
pie	whipped cream	Thanksgiving	dinner
eat	cook	grocery	dairy
meat	fruit	vegetables	appetizers

Vocabulary Cards (words)

turkey	dressing	mashed potatoes	gravy
peas	carrot	roll	butter
pie	whipped cream	Thanksgiving	dinner
eat	cook	grocery	dairy
meat	fruit	vegetables	appetizers

Level: Elementary

Matching

Match the foods that go together.

turkey

peas

mashed potatoes

roll

pie

gravy

whipped cream

dressing

carrot

butter

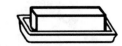

Matching

Match the objects that go together.

shoes

pencil

paper

fork

coat

socks

spoon

toothpaste

toothbrush

cap

Level: Elementary

Complete The Sentence

Cut out the picture symbols at the bottom of the page.
Glue them in the appropriate box to complete the sentence.

mashed potatoes

I like   and ☐ .

turkey

I like   and ☐ .

pie

I like   and ☐ .

peas

I like   and ☐ .

roll

I like   and ☐ .

butter	gravy	whipped cream	dressing	carrot

Count The Cost

Using real coins, match them to the picture symbols below to pay for these items.

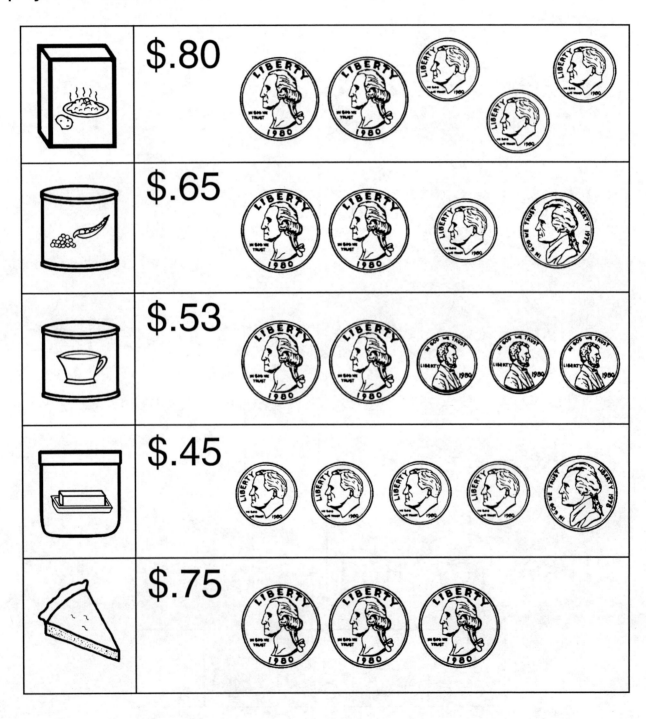

Level: Elementary

What Does It Cost?

Determine the dollar and cents amounts.

 $4.50

 $2.25

 $1.82

 $3.04

Addition Skills

Add up the prices and determine the dollar and cents amounts.

$2.00
+ 1.00
$

$1.00
+ 3.00
$

$4.00
+ 1.00
$

$1.50
+ 2.50
$

$2.50
+ 2.50
$

$3.50
+ 1.50
$

$2.25
+ 1.75
$

$1.25
+ 1.75
$

$3.75
+ 1.25
$

Level: Elementary

Calculator

7	8	9	
4	5	6	-
1	2	3	+
0		.	=

Dollar Patterns

Level: Elementary

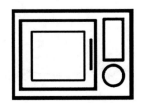

Canned Turkey

 Open the can of turkey.

 Pour it in a bowl.

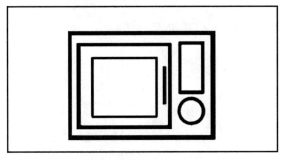 Cook in the microwave for 2 minutes.

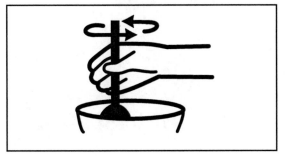 Stir.

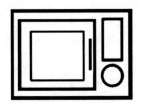

Instant Potatoes

Pour ＿＿＿ cup water in a bowl.

Put ＿＿＿＿＿ salt and ＿＿＿＿ butter in the bowl.

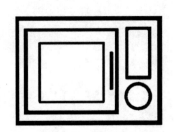

Cook in the microwave for ＿＿＿ minutes.

Pour ＿＿＿ cup milk in the bowl.

Stir in ＿＿＿ cup of instant potatoes.

Level: Elementary

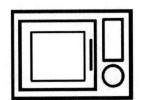 # Canned Gravy

 Pour the gravy in a bowl.

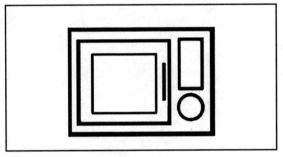 Cook in the microwave for 2 minutes.

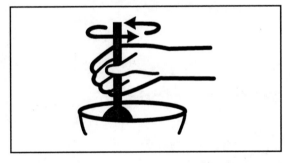 Stir.

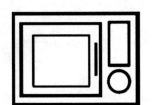

Microwave

1	2
3	4
5	6
7	8	Start
9	0	Cancel

Level: Elementary

Food Wheel

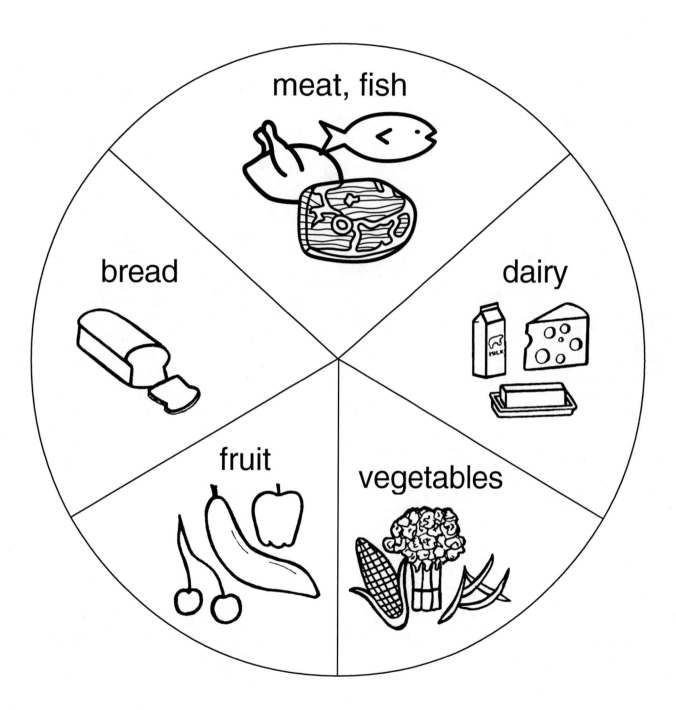

Name _____

Date _____

Unit Topic: Holiday Grooming

Literacy:
- ❑ demonstrates listening and attending behaviors during story reading
- ❑ participates in the story
- ❑ recognizes vocabulary related to holidays
- ❑ identifies Chanukah/Christmas as a holiday
- ❑ identifies labels on grooming products by use
- ❑ reads to follow directions
- ❑ recognizes basic sight words
- ❑ recognizes unit topic sight words
- ❑ applies decoding skills to words and sentences
- ❑ reads prices to $5.00
- ❑ recognizes prices of objects of $5.00 and $10.00
- ❑ locates numbers
    - ❑ calculator

Communication:
- ❑ communicates during activities by _____
- ❑ responds to questions related to unit topic
- ❑ asks questions to gain information
- ❑ conveys personal needs/desires in grooming care

Independent Living:
- ❑ identifies daily grooming tasks
- ❑ participates in daily grooming activities
- ❑ selects clothing appropriate for the occasion
- ❑ recognizes clothing that is clean/dirty

Community Living:
- ❑ shops for personal grooming items
- ❑ uses money to make purchases for items

Recreation/Leisure:
- ❑ participates in holiday related activities
- ❑ participates in holiday decorating activities

Vocational:
- ❑ follows simple directions to complete a task
- ❑ works cooperatively in group activities

Shiny Me

menorah

Christmas tree

Dear Parents:

This month's unit topic includes the Chanukah and Christmas holidays and grooming skills. In our story, the child is preparing for the holidays by looking "shiny and bright." This will include many of the daily cleanliness routines that are practiced in the classroom as well as shower/bathing and clothes selection that is done at home. At home, your child should be encouraged to take an active part in their daily routines. Even a child with physical limitations should begin to realize their own choices in daily grooming and dressing.

During this month, we will focus on vocabulary related to the holidays and grooming. Money skills will be continued on prices of these related objects. Addition and subtraction concepts will be introduced.

Sincerely,

Level: Elementary

The Story: Shiny Tree, Shiny Me

As this story begins, page 138, the Christmas tree is observed after it has been decorated. It is described as "shiny and bright." The story evolves into comparing ourselves in getting ready for Christmas by being shiny and bright. An alternate story, Shiny Candles, Shiny Me, pages 148-156, is included which may be interchanged for the Chanukah season.

Grooming activities are introduced: showering, teeth brushing, hair combing, and dressing in nice, new clothing. Although we take extra time to make ourselves shiny and bright for a special occasion, daily grooming routines are essential for children to learn. However, unlike the shiny and bright holiday decorations, we don't want to be decorated!

Suggested Vocabulary for Reading Activities

Vocabulary Cards (symbols/words), pages 158 and 159, are included for both Christmas and grooming. Alternate Vocabulary Cards (symbols/words), pages 160 and 161, are included for Chanukah. Teaching of these words may be done separately, incorporating a variety of fun holiday activities and relating grooming activities to daily routines.

Grooming vocabulary might be used with the presentation of objects used for grooming. Shampoo, soap, and toothpaste containers may be matched to the symbols or words. Look for these items in store flyers.

Craft making, gift making/giving, and holiday classroom decoration activities may serve as a springboard for use of the suggested holiday vocabulary. Creating cards, whether on the computer or handwritten, will include a variety of literacy skills. Other games and activities may be created with this vocabulary using the Reading/Spelling Activities section, page 5.

Christmas Minibook and Direction Following

The My Christmas Tree minibook, pages 162 and 163, includes sentences that many students may now be able to read independently. These pages involve coloring and adding an object to the Christmas tree on the page. The entire Christmas tree is done on the My Christmas Tree Directions worksheet, page 164.

Students with limited physical ability should have a means to give these directions to another person for completion. Don't forget comments, such as "No, no, not that color."

Daily Grooming and Dressing

Daily grooming activities should be completed in the classroom on a routine basis: face/hand washing, teeth brushing, and hair combing. The classroom setting is not conducive to showering or bathing activities. However, the students may be asked if they did shower or bathe at home, either at night or in the morning. These might be recorded on the I Look Good Every Day chart, page 165. It is important to create an awareness of these grooming activities and the importance that it will have for them

Daily Grooming and Dressing (Cont.)

later in life. Worksheets are included, pages 166 and 167, that provide additional grooming and dressing activities.

Clean clothing should be emphasized, although at this time the students may not have control over this at home. A full-length mirror in the classroom will enable the students to view themselves and make judgments on how they look.

Students who have drool concerns should begin to convey to others when a dry bib is needed. As the child is getting older it might also be time to consider the appropriateness of what the bib is called, i.e. tie, neckerchief, etc. Students should also be encouraged to have control over what clothing choices they wear each day. If parents find this difficult to do in the rush of the morning, then possibly a time might be set aside each evening to determine the clothing to be worn the next day. Parents might offer a choice of two shirts, two pairs of pants, etc. for their child to choose from. Parents should also discuss the weather and occasion for making clothing choices.

In the classroom, clothing choice activities might be introduced. Matching coordinated outfits or sorting by play/dress clothes might be done with clothing brought in. Pictures from catalogs may also be used to match clothing or to identify personal choices for various activities.

Dirty or Clean

Although students may not have direct control over the washing of clothes at home, they should be able to identify clothing that is in need of washing. This might be done in a center type activity using clean shirts/socks/clothing and older stained or painted clothing. This may be a sorting activity, putting the "dirty" clothes in a laundry basket and folding the "clean" clothes. Use the Clean/Dirty Clothing Overlay on page 168.

Students should also begin to identify clothing items that are in need of repair. What means could the student use to let someone know that a button is off or a hole needs to be fixed?

All Dressed Up

Plan a day for students to wear "good" clothing. This might focus around a holiday party or prepare a short program for parents to attend. Such a party might include some food preparation and presentation of a snack to any guests. Having a reason to dress up will give them an example of how these grooming and dressing skills are important.

Addition and Subtraction Skills

Worksheets are included, pages 169-171, that will help introduce or reinforce addition and subtraction concepts. These might serve as a springboard for other story type scenarios that can be used for understanding these concepts. Depending on the students' ability levels, the use of a calculator or development of counting skills may be incorporated.

Money Skills

Students will be taught a variety of levels in understanding money. These may be included in similar activities for students, each understanding different skills.

- Recognize money as used to make purchases. Practice keeping money in a wallet, purse, or fanny pack then getting this money out safely to make a purchase.

- Students should be increasingly aware of the price tag on purchases. Understand the dollar amount and how to determine the needed number of dollars. (The number plus one more.)

- Introduction of the $5 and $10 bills. These are important bills that we keep safe. At first, they are asked to distinguish between the 5 and 10 and matching this to a price tag.

The worksheets included, pages 172 and 173, can serve as practice pages for these money skills when purchasing grooming items or clothing. Further, expansion of these concepts should be involved using real objects, either in a classroom store or in making community purchases. Parents may be asked what brands of shampoo, soap, or toothpaste they use at home and consider sending the money into class to allow the student to go in the community to purchase one or more of these items. If the parents send empty containers of these products, the students may use them to match what they want to buy in the store.

Prices of clothing items may also be identified in department store flyers. This might be done in an activity where they are selecting clothing they like for themselves.

Holiday Shopping

Lists may be obtained from parents if there are small clothing items that the student may purchase for gifts to parents or grandparents. Socks, gloves, handkerchiefs, etc. may be shopped for. Follow up by wrapping and tagging these gifts.

Additional Activity Sources

Storytime, Holiday Fun!, "The Perfect Tree," Creative Communicating.

Hands-on Reading, "Clothing Unit and Hygiene/Body Parts Unit," Mayer-Johnson Co.

More Hands-on Reading, "Corduroy's Christmas," Mayer-Johnson Co.

LIFE, "Shop Til You Drop," Mayer-Johnson Co.

Interactive Augmentative Communication Program, "Holiday Cheer," Creative Communicating.

Shiny Tree, Shiny Me

We have a tree all shiny and bright.
It's decorated for Christmas night.

Christmas tree	shiny and bright	decorate	Christmas night

I want to be shiny and bright.
I want to be ready for Christmas night.

shiny and bright   I'm ready   Christmas night

Level: Elementary

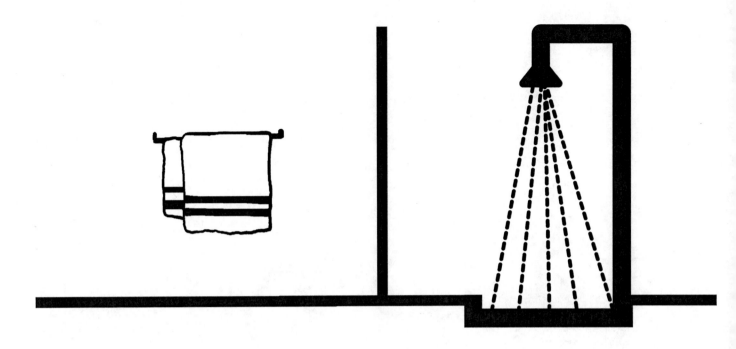

I'll take my shower, rub, rub, rub.
Till I'm shiny and bright
for Christmas night.

shower shiny and bright Christmas night

I'll comb my hair, swish, swish, swish.
Till it's shiny and bright
for Christmas night.

comb hair shiny and bright Christmas night

I'll brush my teeth, brush, brush, brush.
Till they're shiny and bright
for Christmas night.

brush teeth  shiny and bright   Christmas night

I'll put on new clothes, zip, zip, zip.
That are shiny and bright
for Christmas night.

new clothes shiny and bright Christmas night

Level: Elementary

Look at me all shiny and bright.
I'm ready for Christmas night.

shiny and bright	I'm ready	Christmas night

But, please.....
DON'T DECORATE ME!!!

Level: Elementary

Shiny Tree, Shiny Me Overlay

Christmas tree	shiny and bright	Christmas night
shower	comb	brush teeth
new clothes	I'm ready.	Don't decorate me!

Shiny Candles, Shiny Me

We have a menorah all shiny and bright.
It's decorated for Chanukah night.

| menorah | shiny and bright | decorate | Chanukah night |

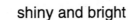

I want to be shiny and bright.
I want to be ready for Chanukah night.

shiny and bright	I'm ready	Chanukah night

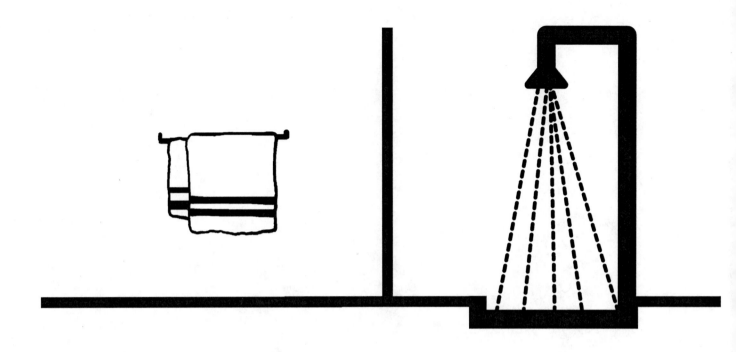

I'll take my shower, rub, rub, rub.
Till I'm shiny and bright
for Chanukah night.

shower   shiny and bright   Chanukah night

I'll comb my hair, swish, swish, swish.
Till it's shiny and bright
for Chanukah night.

comb hair   shiny and bright   Chanukah night

Level: Elementary

I'll brush my teeth, brush, brush, brush.
Till they're shiny and bright
for Chanukah night.

brush teeth   shiny and bright   Chanukah night

I'll put on new clothes, zip, zip, zip.
That are shiny and bright
for Chanukah night.

new clothes   shiny and bright   Chanukah night

Look at me all shiny and bright.
I'm ready for Chanukah night.

shiny and bright   I'm ready   Chanukah night

But, please.....
DON'T DECORATE ME!!!

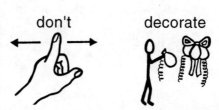

don't   decorate

Level: Elementary

Shiny Candles, Shiny Me Overlay

menorah	shiny and bright	Chanukah night
comb	comb	brush teeth
new clothes	I'm ready.	Don't decorate me!

Vocabulary Cards (symbols)

Christmas	tree	present	wreath
stocking	ball	lights	bells
shower	comb	brush	clothes
shirt	pants	dress	shoes
toothpaste	towel	soap	shampoo

Level: Elementary

Vocabulary Cards (words)

Christmas	tree	present	wreath
stocking	ball	lights	bells
shower	comb	brush	clothes
shirt	pants	dress	shoes
toothpaste	towel	soap	shampoo

Vocabulary Cards (symbols)

Chanukah	menorah	candle	latke
gelt	hora	dreidel	decorate
shower	comb	brush	clothes
shirt	pants	dress	shoes
toothpaste	towel	soap	shampoo

Level: Elementary

Vocabulary Cards (words)

Chanukah	menorah	candle	latke
gelt	hora	dreidel	decorate
shower	comb	brush	clothes
shirt	pants	dress	shoes
toothpaste	towel	soap	shampoo

My Christmas Tree

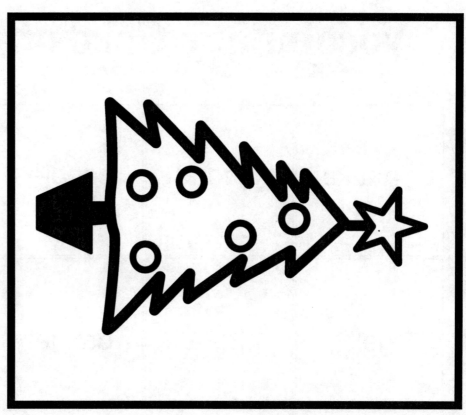

Red balls are on the tree.

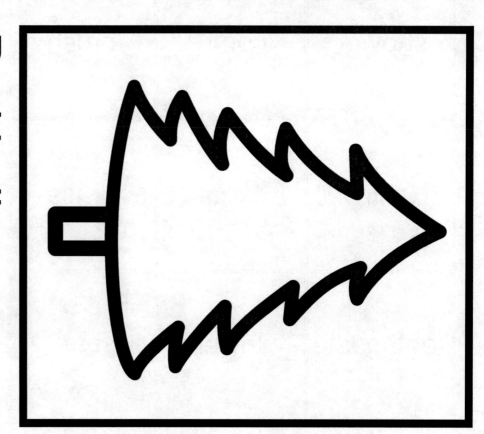

Level: Elementary

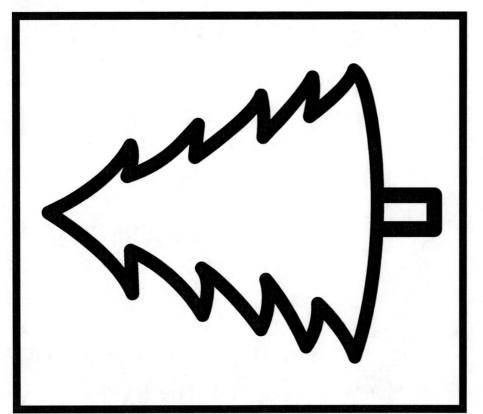

A present for me is under the tree.

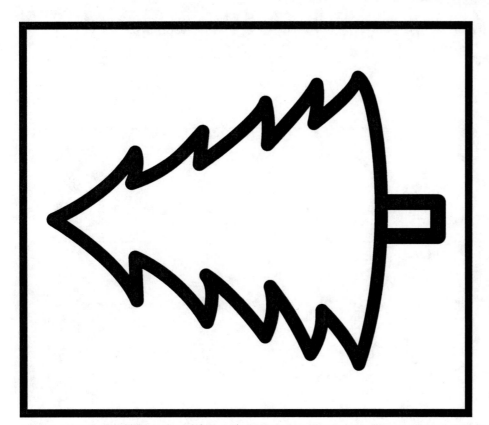

A yellow star is on top of the tree.

My Christmas Tree Directions

1. Color the tree green.

2. Put red balls on the tree.

3. Put a yellow star on top of the tree.

4. Put the present under the tree.

Use this set of symbols to put in the minibook story.

 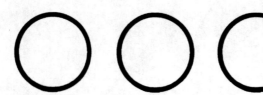 

Level: Elementary

I Look Good Every Day

Record daily grooming activities below.

Complete The Sentence

Cut out the picture symbols at the bottom of the page.
Glue them in the box next to the appropriate sentence.

I have new shoes.

I comb my hair.

I take my shower.

I put on new clothes.

I brush my teeth.

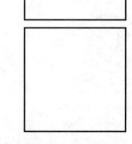

brush	comb	shower	clothes	shoes
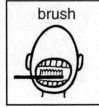				

Level: Elementary

Grooming And Dressing

What do you need to....

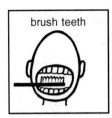 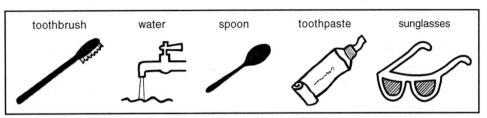

| brush teeth | toothbrush | water | spoon | toothpaste | sunglasses |

 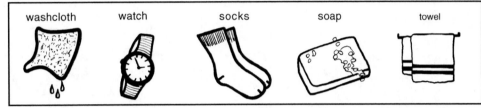

| take a shower | washcloth | watch | socks | soap | towel |

 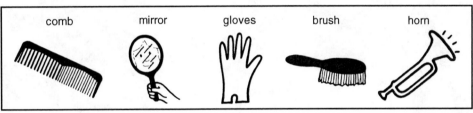

| comb hair | comb | mirror | gloves | brush | horn |

What will you put on?

 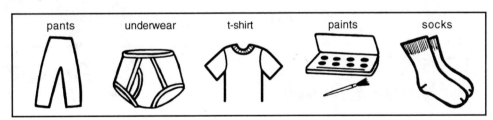

| put on | pants | underwear | t-shirt | paints | socks |

What will you eat for breakfast?

| breakfast | cereal | pancakes | salad | fried egg | popcorn |

Clean/Dirty Clothing Overlay

clean   dirty

Addition Skills

How many presents?

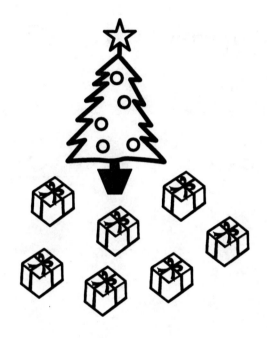

Alysha   2

Katie   2

Kelly   +3
_____

How many balls?

red balls   4

yellow balls   3

blue balls   +2
_____

Addition Skills

How many presents?

Alysha	2
Katie	2
Kelly	+3

How many dreidels?

red dreidels	4
yellow dreidels	3
blue dreidels	+2

Subtraction Skills

Brent has 5 shirts.

$$\begin{array}{r} 5 \\ -\ 2 \\ \hline \end{array}$$

2 shirts are dirty.
How many shirts are clean?

Ted has 6 cookies.

$$\begin{array}{r} 6 \\ -\ 4 \\ \hline \end{array}$$

He eats 4 cookies.
How many are left?

What Does It Cost?

How many dollars do you need?

$3.75

$1.59

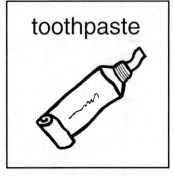

$2.38

$1.46

Level: Elementary

What Does It Cost?

How many dollars do you need?

$5.00

$10.00

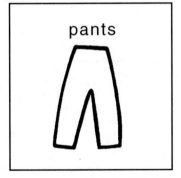

$10.00

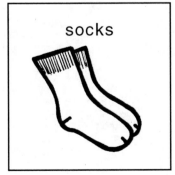

$5.00

Name _____

Date _____

Unit Topic: This Is Me

Literacy:

- ❑ demonstrates listening and attending behaviors during story reading
- ❑ participates in the story
- ❑ recognizes personal ID information:
    - ❑ name ❑ sex ❑ city
    - ❑ siblings ❑ parents
- ❑ recognizes personal characteristics:
    - ❑ hair color ❑ eye color
- ❑ recognizes living accommodations
- ❑ recognizes personal favorites:
    - ❑ color ❑ food ❑ TV show ❑ music
- ❑ recognizes basic sight words
- ❑ recognizes unit topic sight words
- ❑ recognizes initial letters/sounds in words
- ❑ copies/writes/types unit words
- ❑ counts objects/identifies number
- ❑ has been introduced to addition concepts

Communication:

- ❑ communicates during activities by _____
- ❑ asks questions to gain information
- ❑ responds to questions related to topic activities
- ❑ states personal ID information

Independent/Community Living:

- ❑ responds to requests for personal information appropriately
- ❑ determines own personal preferences
- ❑ states city of residence

Recreation/Leisure:

- ❑ identifies activities of choice
- ❑ participates in group gross motor games

Vocational:

- ❑ follows simple directions in classroom activities
- ❑ completes assignments with minimal prompts

Level: Elementary

This Is Me!

I, me

Dear Parents:

This month's topic is entitled "This Is Me." During this unit we will discover the similarities and differences among all of us — the things that make us special. We will create a book that includes each person's physical characteristics, family members, and personal favorites. To help us identify these, there is a home questionnaire attached. Please complete this form and return it to school as soon as possible.

Each student will have a day to call his/her own. On each child's special day, they may bring in pictures, toys, or other personal favorites that they would like to share with the class.

Sincerely,

Level: Elementary

Name_____

Date_____

Home Questionnaire

Please complete this form to help us know your child better. This information will be used in a variety of classroom activities, as well as in creating communication books and displays. Photographs are always appreciated.

Thank you for your time in completing this and returning it to school.

Family members:

Name	Age	Relationship	Lives in home?
_____	_____	_____	_____
_____	_____	_____	_____
_____	_____	_____	_____
_____	_____	_____	_____
_____	_____	_____	_____
_____	_____	_____	_____

Other special adults or peers in your child's life: (state name and relationship)

Pets: (type/name)

Activities your child enjoys:

Activities your child dislikes:

Foods your child likes:

Foods your child dislikes:

Community places your child goes to frequently:

Favorites:

    color   _____

    food   _____

    drink   _____

    kind of music _____

    song   _____

    TV show(s) _____

    fast food restaurant(s) _____

    sports _____

    sports teams _____

Other special things that make your child unique:

The Story: This Is Me

This story, pages 181-190, introduces a boy and a girl, each different — but both very special. It serves as the springboard for discussion on things that are different about each of the students in the class. The story will also develop into the students' own book that includes the color of their hair and eyes, where they live, family members, and personal favorites.

Information obtained from the home questionnaire will enable the classroom activities to focus on the personal items of each student. The This Is Me Overlay, page 191, with the story may be customized for each student.

Basic identifying information should be included on other communication devices that the student may have.

Suggested Vocabulary for Reading Activities

The suggested vocabulary list includes family members, housing locations, and samples of favorite foods and activities. Recognition of vocabulary should be added to include the names of family members, the city where the child lives, and his/her own personal favorites.

The Vocabulary Cards (symbols/words), pages 192 and 193, may be sorted into categories using the four category pictures on the Sorting worksheet, page 194, as a guide: places we live, people in our family, things we like to do, and food we eat. Customize by adding the student's personal information.

Use the suggestions in the Reading/Spelling Activities section, page 5, to create reading and spelling games with the words for this unit.

Words should be combined into simple sentences for reading. The starter phrase "This is" may be used in conjunction with several other vocabulary words.

This Is Me Book

Each student should have the opportunity to create the This Is Me book, pages 195-199. Photos may be requested from home or taken with a classroom camera. Under each picture the blanks should be completed with child specific information. This also provides the students a chance to ask questions of each other: "Where do you live?" "Do you have any brothers?" "What is your favorite food?" Encourage student interaction and comments during these activities.

Each student may use the This Is Me Overlay, page 191, to tell about him/herself. This introduction may be videotaped for later viewing or sharing with home. Or each student may be interviewed and videotaped.

Additional worksheets are included, pages 200 and 201, that provide matching activities.

Math Activities

Students may incorporate many types of graph ideas this month, i.e. identifying students by the color of their hair, the color of their eyes, where they live, their favorite colors, their favorite foods, etc. These facilitate counting as well as the concepts of more and less. Graphs are included for hair and eye color, pages 202 and 203. Students' names or pictures may be attached to the graph for recording purposes. Similar graphs may be made to include other concepts for comparison.

Addition concepts are also introduced on the My Family and Classmates' Families worksheets, pages 204 and 205, to identify how many people are in each person's family. Students may share this information with the class. Who has the most people in their family? Who has the most sisters? Who has no brothers?

My Special Day

Each student may be selected as the special student of the day. On this day, the student may bring in special things from home to share with the class. Parents or family members may also want to visit on this day. Photos may be placed on a special bulletin board.

On this special day, prepare the student's favorite food for lunch or snack.

Guess Who I Am?

Trace silhouettes of the students using a light or overhead projector. Students should write or type information to attach to the silhouette for others to guess who it is.

I have _____ hair and _____ eyes.

I live in _____.

My favorite food is _____.

I like to _____.

Who am I?

This information may also be included on an enlarged keyboard and sentences typed by activating symbol spaces.

Paper Plate Faces

Each student may create his/her face, starting with a paper plate. Add eyes that are the same color as the student. Add other features. Include hair from pieces of yarn to match the student's hair color and length.

Additional Activity Sources

Interactive Augmentative Communication Program, "All About Me," Mayer-Johnson Co.

More Hands-on Reading, "Family Fun Unit," Mayer-Johnson Co.

This Is Me

I am a boy.
I have brown hair and brown eyes.
This is me.

brown   hair   eyes

I am a girl.
I have blonde hair and blue eyes.
This is me.

blonde   hair   blue   eyes

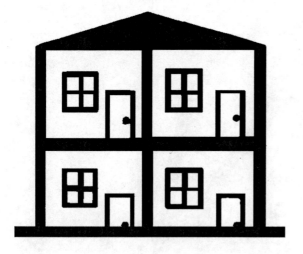

I live in an apartment
with my mom and sister.
This is me.

apartment   family

Level: Elementary

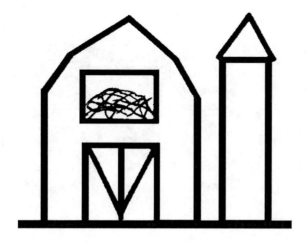

I live on a farm
with my mom and dad
and my little brother.
This is me.

farm

family

I like to play baseball
and ride my bike.
This is me.

baseball   bicycle

Level: Elementary

I like to listen to music
and watch TV.
This is me.

listen to music   watch

My favorite food is pizza.
This is me.

pizza

Level: Elementary

My favorite food is fried chicken.
This is me.

chicken

We are all different.
We are all so special.
I am glad to say,
"This is ME."

special

me

Level: Elementary

This Is Me Overlay

This is me. 	I am........	I have........hair. 
I have........eyes. 	I live........ 	with........ 
I like to........ 	My favorite food is.... 	I am special because... 

Vocabulary Cards (symbols)

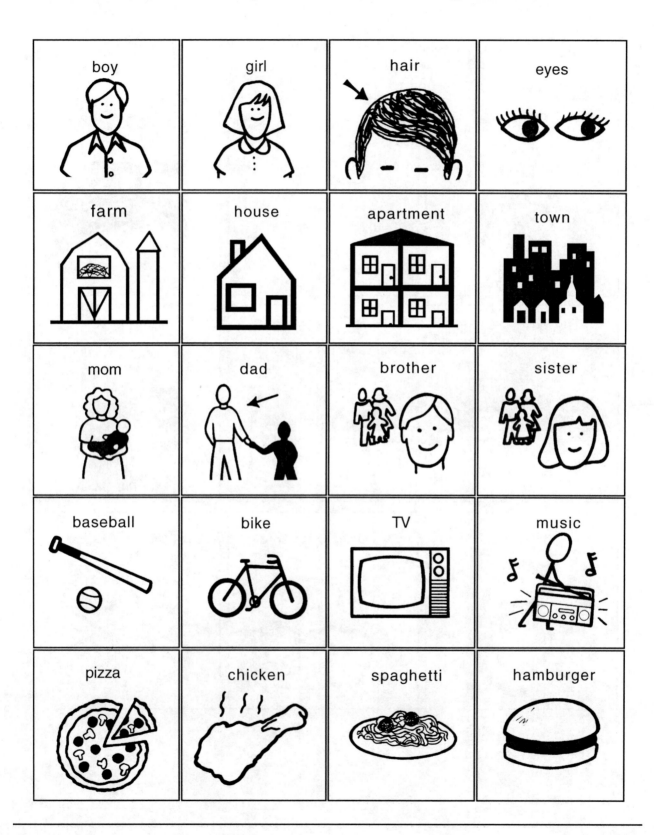

boy	girl	hair	eyes
farm	house	apartment	town
mom	dad	brother	sister
baseball	bike	TV	music
pizza	chicken	spaghetti	hamburger

Level: Elementary

Vocabulary Cards (words)

boy	girl	hair	eyes
farm	house	apartment	town
mom	dad	brother	sister
baseball	bike	TV	music
pizza	chicken	spaghetti	hamburger

Sorting

Sort the vocabulary cards into these categories.

Places we live.	People in our family.
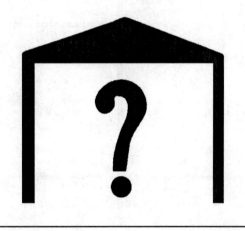	
Things we like to do.	Food we eat.
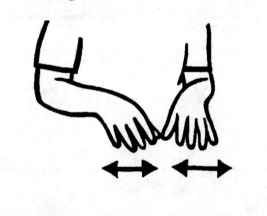	

This Is Me

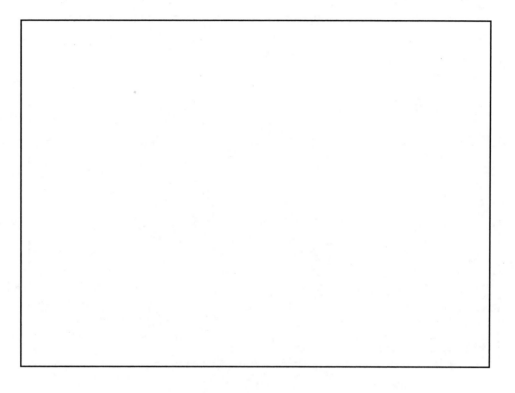

I am a _____.

I have _____hair

and _____ eyes.

_____

This is my family and me.

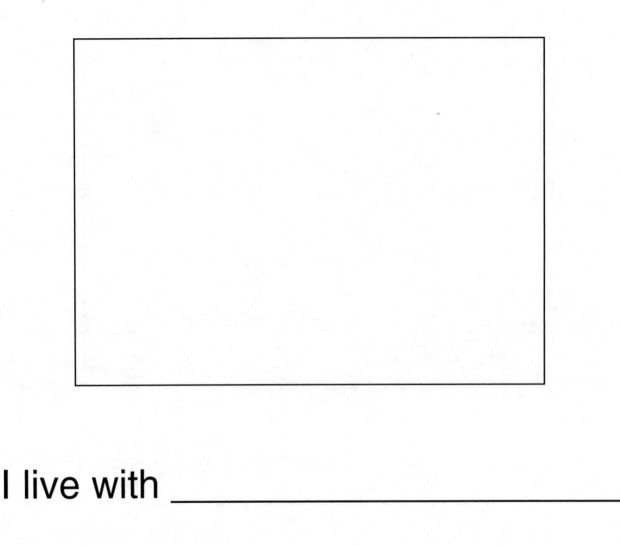

I live with _____

_____.

I have _____ brothers and

_____ sisters.

Level: Elementary

This is where I live.

I live in _____.

My house is _____

_____.

These are my favorites.

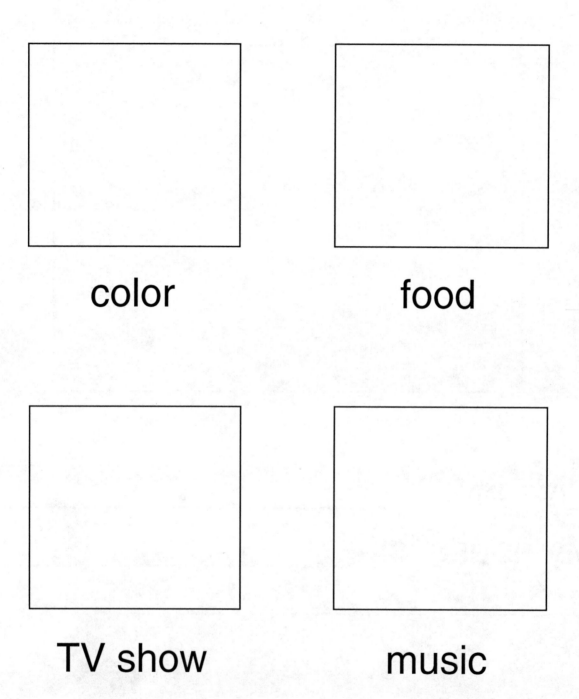

color

food

TV show

music

These are more things I like.

I am a very special person!

Matching

Match the sentence to the picture symbol.

This is me.

This is mom.

This is dad.

This is brother.

This is sister.

Matching

Match the places people live.

farm

apartment

house

town

apartment

farm

town

house

Hair Color Graph

brown	blonde	black	red

Eye Color Graph

brown	blue	gray	green

My Family

Count the boys and/or girls in your family.

Level: Elementary

Classmates' Families

Count the boys and/or girls in your classmates' families.

Name _____

```
  [ ]      boys
+ [ ]      girls
─────
  [ ]
```

Name _____

```
  [ ]      boys
+ [ ]      girls
─────
  [ ]
```

Name _____

```
  [ ]      boys
+ [ ]      girls
─────
  [ ]
```

Name _____

```
  [ ]      boys
+ [ ]      girls
─────
  [ ]
```

Name _____

Date _____

Unit Topic: Help At Home

Literacy:

- ❏ demonstrates listening and attending behaviors during story reading
- ❏ participates in the story
- ❏ differentiates work/non-work activities
- ❏ identifies rooms in the house
- ❏ identifies specific home jobs
- ❏ follows directions related to jobs
- ❏ identifies basic sight words
- ❏ identifies unit topic sight words
- ❏ recognizes initial letters and sounds in words
- ❏ copies/writes/types unit words
- ❏ identifies time
    - ❏ hour   ❏ half-hour

Communication:

- ❏ communicates during activities by _____
- ❏ asks questions to gain information
- ❏ responds to questions related to topic activities
- ❏ requests assistance

Independent/Community Living:

- ❏ identifies jobs that can be done at home
- ❏ participates in routine of home help activities
- ❏ establishes a routine of home help jobs
- ❏ recognizes responsibility to help at home

Recreation/Leisure:

- ❏ participates in home leisure activities
- ❏ identifies choices in home leisure activities

Vocational:

- ❏ follows a sequence of jobs to be completed
- ❏ recognizes that work must be completed before leisure

Help At Home

Dear Parents:

This month's unit is entitled "Help At Home" and will explore various jobs that the student might do at home to help. Samples of these jobs will be incorporated into our reading and math activities. If your child has routine jobs at home now, it may be helpful to let us know what they are and what other jobs you feel your child might be able to learn as time goes on.

It is important that children recognize home responsibilities and that jobs must be completed before play time. Early experiences will lead to lifetime habits and greater independence as an adult.

For our students with limited physical abilities, we must emphasize the importance of being a part of the home and their own care. Sometimes this comes in the form of letting others know what they need in an appropriate manner. We may also explore ways that environmental tasks can be performed through the use of switches.

Sincerely,

Level: Elementary

The Story: I Can Help

This story, pages 211-218, involves helping jobs that are done in various rooms of the home and various times of the week. The children in the story are demonstrating what jobs they can do all by themselves. The story might serve as an introduction to find out what jobs are expected of the students at home. It is also a time to encourage parents to assign jobs to their children.

Students with physical limitations can realize that they may help by conveying basic needs to others. This is also a time to investigate environmental control type systems that might enable the individual to get more involved in their own routine at home.

As with any child, the earlier he/she can learn to accept responsibilities, the more likely he/she is to "want" these responsibilities later in life. At home, it is likely easier to just do it than get the child involved in learning household tasks. This unit may help encourage parents that the end result of giving their child routine jobs will have long-term gains for them.

Suggested Vocabulary for Reading Activities

The Vocabulary Cards (symbols/words) included, pages 220 and 221, are both work and non-work related words that occur at home. Some words are noun-based words, however they reflect an action or task that can be done, i.e. "music" refers to listening to music.

These words can also be simulated in classroom activities. The words and activities may be incorporated into centers or group tasks, with emphasis on a work-related task being completed before the non-work related task, i.e. set the table, then eat. A Sorting worksheet, page 222, is included.

Use the suggestions in the Reading/Spelling Activities section, page 5, to create reading and spelling games with the words for this unit. Students with limited physical ability should be presented reading activities in adapted modes and/or by using communication devices.

Sentence matching activities, pages 223 and 224, are included. The carrier phrase "I can..." is used with these sentences.

Rooms in the House

Four rooms are identified in the story: the living room, bedroom, kitchen, and laundry room. Create a sorting activity with the worksheets on pages 225 and 226 by having the students sort the furniture, objects, and appliances that are found in each room. Discuss the use of each object in the room. Further expansion of this activity may be done by sorting pictures from catalogs. Students may also select the types of furniture/objects that they would prefer if designing their own room.

Time Activities

Several worksheets are included, pages 227-229, that will introduce time concepts. Time to the hour and half-hour may be explored depending on the student's level. Include digital clock work if appropriate.

One worksheet, Telling Time, page 229, is left blank. This page may be laminated. Velcro® a vocabulary card on the action square and the time may be added by drawing hands on the clock with a dry erase marker.

Certain jobs may be located on the days of the week and attached to the calendar. Emphasis on all time activities should reflect work first then we play.

Work Schedules

A sample work schedule entitled My Jobs For Today is included, page 230. This, too, may be laminated and then Velcro® jobs onto the "Do" side. When the job is done, the card is transferred to the "Done" side. This can serve as a job chart for home and/or school. School related symbols may be added as well as job related tasks.

During all activities, the students should be encouraged to request assistance as needed. They may also need to report when a job is all done. These symbols are included on the job chart.

Recreation/Leisure Activities

Throughout this month, indoor recreation activities may be explored. Again, the emphasis is on work first, then play. Choices of activities should be presented. Listening to music, reading a book, playing a game, watching TV, etc. are all typical home leisure activities. Add other activities that are specific to the students' interests.

Recreation activities should be adapted for students with limited physical abilities. Explore the possibilities for environmental control.

Additional Activity Sources

More Hands-on Reading, "A Clean House for Mole and Mouse," page 121, Mayer-Johnson Co.

I Can Help

So many jobs at home to do.
Can you help?
Is there a job just for you?

Can you?   help

In the kitchen, I can help.
I set the table
all by myself!

kitchen 　　help 　　set table 　　I can

In the living room, I can help.
I vacuum the floor
all by myself!

living room	help	vacuum	I can
	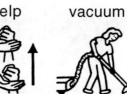		

Level: Elementary

In the bedroom, I can help.
I make my bed
all by myself!

bedroom   help   make bed   I can

On laundry day, I can help.
I fold the towels
all by myself!

laundry day

help

fold

I can

Level: Elementary

On trash day, I can help.
I take out the trash
all by myself!

trash day   help   take trash out   I can

So many jobs at home to do.
I can help.
How about you?

help   Can you?

Level: Elementary

I Can Help Overlay

I can	help	Can you?
vacuum floor	make bed	set table
take trash out	fold laundry	prepare lunch

Vocabulary Cards (symbols)

vacuum	bed	table	trash
laundry	lunch	help	clean
watch	music	play	read
rest	drink	eat	sleep
		more	done

Level: Elementary

Vocabulary Cards (words)

vacuum	bed	table	trash
laundry	lunch	help	clean
watch	music	play	read
rest	drink	eat	sleep
		more	done

Sorting

Sort the vocabulary cards according to what is work, and what activities can be done after the work is done.

Level: Elementary

Complete The Sentence

Cut out the picture symbols at the bottom of the page.
Glue them in the box next to the appropriate sentence.

I can <u>vacuum</u> the floor.

I can set the <u>table</u>.

I can make my <u>bed</u>.

I can help with <u>lunch</u>.

I can fold the <u>laundry</u>.

| lunch | vacuum | make bed | laundry | set table |

Matching

Match the action to the picture symbol.

I can eat.

I can rest.

I can drink.

I can sleep.

I can play.

Level: Elementary

Sorting

Sort the objects from page 226 into each room below.

kitchen	living room

bedroom	**laundry room**

Sorting

couch

dresser

lamp

dryer

laundry

microwave

washer

refrigerator

sink

bed

TV

chair

Level: Elementary

Telling Time

Kelly will make her bed and clean her bedroom at 10:00.

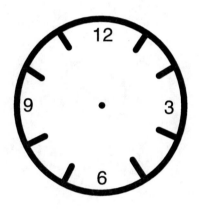 

Then she can watch TV at 11:00.

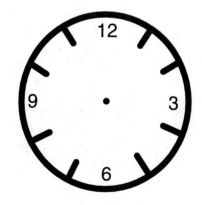 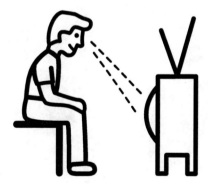

Telling Time

Andy can take out the trash at 1:00.

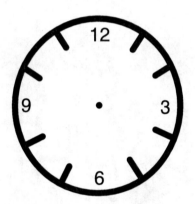 

Then he can listen to music at 1:30.

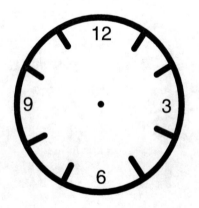 

Level: Elementary

Telling Time

Laminate. Attach a job, tell what time.

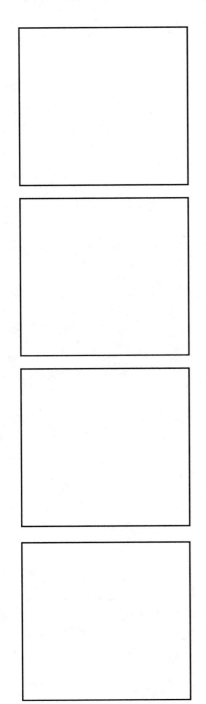

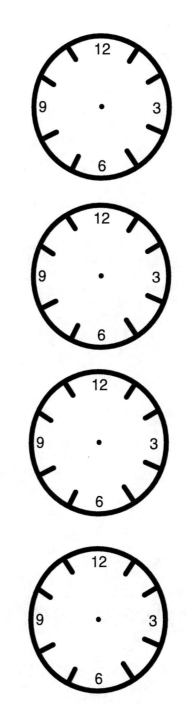

My Jobs For Today

Do	Done 

I need more	I need help

Level: Elementary

Name _____

Date _____

Unit Topic: Community Helpers

Literacy:
- ❑ demonstrates listening and attending behaviors during story reading
- ❑ participates in the story
- ❑ recognizes community locations
- ❑ identifies community helpers
- ❑ identifies jobs associated with community helpers
- ❑ recognizes basic sight words
- ❑ recognizes unit topic sight words
- ❑ applies decoding skills to words and sentences
- ❑ locates numbers in phone numbers
- ❑ applies addition concepts
- ❑ tells time of appointments
    - ❑ hour   ❑ half-hour   ❑ day

Communication:
- ❑ communicates during activities by _____
- ❑ demonstrates social etiquette
    - ❑ thank you   ❑ greetings
- ❑ requests assistance in community settings
- ❑ conveys message on the telephone

Independent Living:
- ❑ identifies personal needs from community persons
- ❑ recognizes name of personal doctor and dentist
- ❑ recognizes personal safety in the community

Community Living:
- ❑ cares for own belongings when traveling in the community
- ❑ uses money to make purchases
- ❑ demonstrates appropriate behaviors in the community

Recreation/Leisure:
- ❑ participates in community leisure activities
    - ❑ library   ❑ eating out   ❑ shopping

Vocational:
- ❑ recognizes the jobs of community helpers
- ❑ has developed a desire to work as an adult

Community Helpers

city

Dear Parents:

Our new unit discusses the many community workers and locations where we might find help. We will discover places where we go for health, leisure, and routine services. As we learn about these people we begin to instill a desire that the students will want to work at a job some day also. We may go into the community and/or have community people visit in our classroom.

This unit will continue to apply many of our reading and math skills. We will use numbers for an introduction to the telephone and in telling time. Word recognition is important in knowing the places we go to in the community.

Sincerely,

Level: Elementary

The Story: I Go To Town

This story, pages 236-246, involves a young man who is going to town on Saturday. Along the way he stops at several places: the library, the grocery store, the doctor's office, and a restaurant. At each place, someone asks "Can I help you?" This offers the opportunity to discuss the possible things we might need assistance with in each location. At the end of the story, the boy states that he would like to be a "helper" when he grows up. This unit should serve as a means to spark the students' interest in wanting to be something when they grow up.

This unit will continue to introduce other community helpers. Depending on the setup of each specific classroom, the activities may be branched into real community sites or simulated in the classroom setting.

Suggested Vocabulary for Reading Activities

The Vocabulary Cards (symbols/words), pages 248 and 249, selected for this unit include community persons and locations. Understanding may be enhanced through purposeful trips to these locations. Examples might include:

- Go to the drugstore and buy a greeting card. Address the card to a family member or classmate. Go to the post office to buy a stamp and mail the card.
- Go to the local library. Select a book to share with the class. Return the book on another day.
- Go out to eat for lunch. Plan what restaurant you will go to and decide on food choices.
- Go to the barber shop and make an appointment for a haircut.

Remember that class outings are more natural if done in small groups. Limit the number of students traveling to a site to one or two at a time. If it is difficult to get students with physical involvement out into the community, simulate the setting in the classroom.

Some of the vocabulary is conducive to inviting the community helper into the classroom. A doctor, dentist, nurse, or dental hygienist may visit and do class presentations or health screenings.

Classroom centers may be arranged with various community locations. Remember to put the store or office name and symbol by it. Create role-playing activities.

Several literacy worksheets are included, pages 250-252, that will get the students to work with the vocabulary in sentence and symbol forms.

Further reading and writing activities may be created with these words and cards using the suggestions in the Reading/Spelling Activities section, page 5.

Math Activities

Presentation of numbers and math concepts may be integrated into many activities. Seek ways to utilize these numbers in all situations. An Addition Skills worksheet, page 253, is included to reinforce the counting and adding skills that the students have learned.

Telephoning Skills

Numbers are also presented in telephone numbers. While the students are too young to be making their own doctor and dentist appointments, it is not too soon to begin recognizing the numbers used for telephoning. Cards are included, page 254, for identifying their personal doctor or dentist and their phone numbers. A large paper telephone is included, page 255, for practice locating these numbers in a sequence.

Students with physical limitations should be encouraged to locate the numbers in sequence through scanning techniques.

The phone card may be laminated for use with other practice activities. Disconnected phones may also be used for these activities with simulated phone conversations. Students should learn basic phone etiquette, such as "hello" and how to respond to a caller. Each student's individual ability and curiosity should be considered when teaching phone skills. Stress the importance in adult supervision when making phone calls.

Making Appointments

While some community locations can be visited without notice, others require an appointment. This unit may serve as an introduction to this distinction. Going to various community stores/offices must also be planned. The classroom calendar may be used for identifying the dates/days that students may be going out to a community location. Symbol cards may be attached to the calendar with a time also. These can be reviewed each day during the circle time activities.

Worksheets are included, pages 256 and 257, for recognition of days and time.

Communicating in the Community

Whenever the students travel into community settings they should have an adequate means to greet others or request assistance in whatever task they are attempting. For many students this may mean the use of communication boards, books, or devices. The use of these will not stifle their attempts to verbalize. It will provide them with an understandable means to complete the task with more independence. If a student is using a communication aid, they should practice this in simulated classroom activities prior to going out.

Community persons also need to be educated on the way that students can use their communication aid. Adult persons accompanying the student should employ tactful strategies to allow the student to speak for themselves.

Level: Elementary

Community Safety

It is also important to review community safety rules for traveling in the community (page 258). There are numerous strangers when out and about. While we want to encourage a friendly attitude, students need to be cautious of strangers who offer them a ride or other things. Emphasize the importance of staying with the person who is accompanying them from home or school.

Additional Activity Sources

Units, "Community Workers," Mayer-Johnson Co.

Interactive Augmentative Communication Program, "Our Community," Mayer-Johnson Co.

I Go To Town

Level: Elementary

Saturday is fun
because that's the day
I go to town.

Saturday fun town

I go to the library.
Harriet, the librarian, puts away books.
She says, "Can I help you?"

library

librarian

help

I ask her to help me find
a book about rabbits.
"Thank you."

help   book   thank you

Groceries

I go to the grocery store.
Lisa, the clerk, is at the cash register.
She says, "Can I help you?"

grocery store   clerk   help

Level: Elementary

Groceries

I ask her to help me find
some cheese.
"Thank you."

help   cheese   thank you

I go to the doctor's office.
Cindy, the nurse, is helping a patient.
She says, "Can I help you?"

help   nurse

Level: Elementary

Not today.
I'm not sick.
"Goodbye."

not   sick   goodbye

I go to the restaurant.
Donnie, the server, is waiting for me.
He says, "Can I help you?"

restaurant   server   help

Level: Elementary

I ask him for
a hamburger and soda, please.
"Thank you."

hamburger   soda   thank you

When I get big,
I want to help people too.
I can already say, "Can I help you?"

help

Level: Elementary

I Go To Town Overlay

I go to 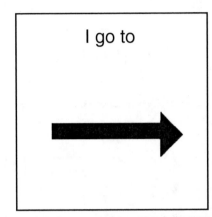	town 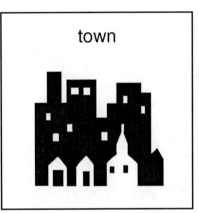	library 
grocery store 	doctor's office 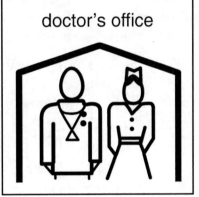	restaurant 
Can I help you? 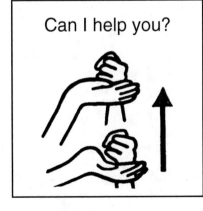	thank you 	goodbye 

Vocabulary Cards (symbols)

town	library	restaurant	doctor's office
grocery store	drugstore	department sto	post office
nurse	doctor	dentist	waitress
clerk	barber	bank teller	worker
janitor	stranger	thank you	goodbye

Level: Elementary

Vocabulary Cards (words)

town	library	restaurant	doctor's office
grocery store	drugstore	department store	post office
nurse	doctor	dentist	waitress
clerk	barber	bank teller	worker
janitor	stranger	thank you	goodbye

Complete The Sentence

Cut out the picture symbols at the bottom of the page.
Glue them in the box next to the appropriate sentence.

I go to the restaurant.

I go to the library.

I go to the doctor's office.

I go to town.

I go to the grocery store.

library	doctor's office	town	grocery store	restaurant

Level: Elementary

What Will They Use At Work?

Circle the items that each community helper uses.

nurse	thermometer	tire	stethoscope
barber	whistle	razor	scissors
janitor	broom	brush & pail	camera
waitress	glass	ladder	menu
bank teller	money	check	basket

Where Can You Buy It?

Circle the place where you can buy each item.

french fries	restaurant	drugstore	grocery store
medicine	doctor's office	drugstore	department sto
shirt	grocery store	restaurant	department sto
stamp	doctor's office	drugstore	post office
video tape	department sto	grocery store	post office

Level: Elementary

Addition Skills

Count the number of books for each person.
Add up the total number of books.

Randy

Ryan

Mary Beth

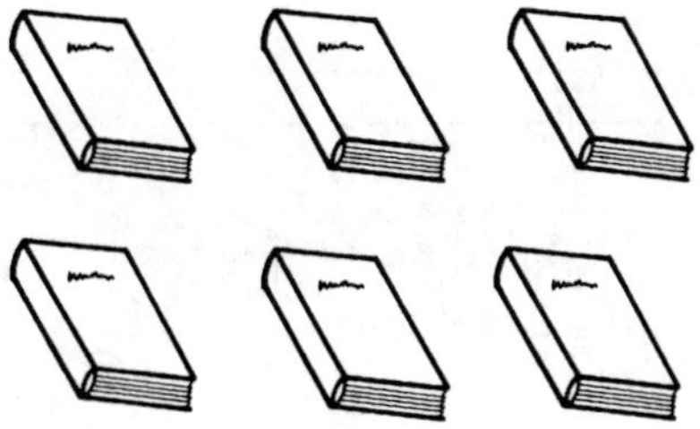

Danielle

+

How many books all together?

Telephone Skills

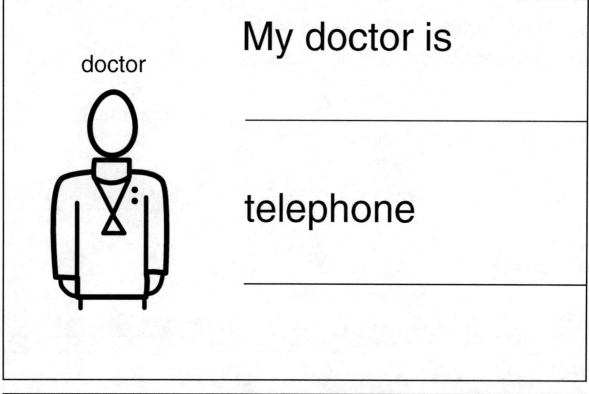

doctor

My doctor is

_____

telephone

_____

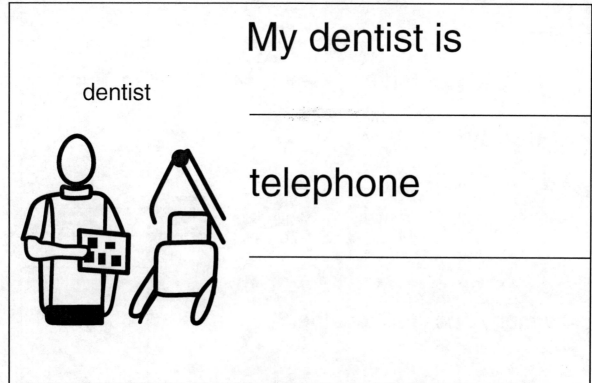

dentist

My dentist is

_____

telephone

_____

Level: Elementary

Telephone

1	2	3
4	5	6
7	8	9
*	0	#

hello

goodbye

Matching

Match the appointment to the day of the week.

On Saturday,
I go to town.

On Tuesday,
I go to the dentist.

On Monday,
I go to the bank.

On Friday,
I go to the grocery store.

On Wednesday,
I go to the doctor.

On Thursday,
I go out to eat.

(On Sunday, I rest.)

Monday

Tuesday

Wednesday

Thursday

Friday

Saturday

Level: Elementary

Telling Time

Draw the hands on the clock to match the time.

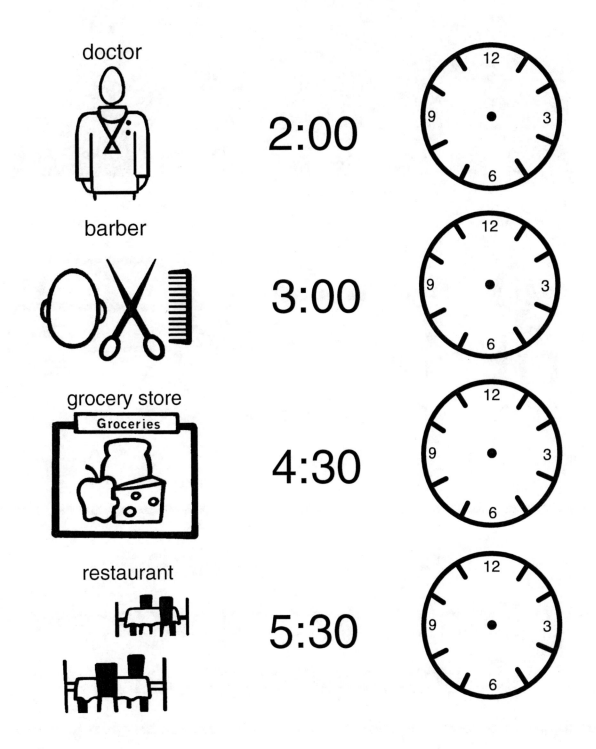

doctor

2:00

barber

3:00

grocery store

Groceries

4:30

restaurant

5:30

Community Safety

Stay with a friend.
Don't talk to strangers.
Don't go in a car.

Level: Elementary

Name_____

Date_____

Unit Topic: Transportation

Literacy:

❑ demonstrates listening and attending behaviors during story reading
❑ participates in the story
❑ identifies vehicles
❑ recognizes locations associated with vehicles
❑ sorts items by categories
❑ introduces alphabetical order
❑ recognizes basic sight words
❑ applies decoding skills to words and sentences
❑ locates numbers in phone numbers
❑ applies time/money concepts

Communication:

❑ communicates during activities by _____
❑ shares information about a trip
❑ asks questions to gain information

Independent/Community Living:

❑ cares for own belongings when traveling
❑ identifies home town
❑ recognizes towns of others
❑ uses seat belt when traveling

Recreation/Leisure:

❑ identifies personal vacation trips
❑ demonstrates turn taking in game playing activities
❑ explores recreation riding vehicles

Vocational:

❑ works cooperatively in group activities
❑ has developed an awareness of jobs related to care of vehicles

Level: Elementary   259

Transportation

trip

Dear Parents:

This unit focuses on different forms of transportation. The story with this unit is called "Taking A Trip." We will explore the various vehicles that might be taken on a trip. If your family has taken a special vacation, please send in some pictures that can be shared with the class. We enjoy sharing these experiences and asking questions about these trips.

During this unit, we will plan some of our own trips — some imaginary and some real field trips. In planning trips, we will need to determine how we will travel, when we will leave, and what we will need to pack for the trip. This will enable us to practice many of our reading and math skills.

Sincerely,

Level: Elementary

The Story: Taking A Trip

In this story, pages 264-275, various forms of transportation are explored. The boy in the story wants to take a trip and he decides on places he might go and ways to get there. These may serve as starters for the children to discuss places they have traveled to and vehicles they have traveled in. At the end of the story, the boy decides to take a trip on his bicycle, while pretending he is on the airplane, bus, car, and boat. This unit may develop into several areas, such as taking field trips and discussing vacations.

Suggested Vocabulary for Reading Activities

The Vocabulary Cards (symbols/words), pages 277 and 278, selected for this unit include a variety of vehicles. Several of these may be simulated in classroom activities by lining up chairs. Pretend these chairs are a bus, airplane, boat, or car. (Don't forget to leave room for wheelchairs.) Students can pretend to take a trip, entering and exiting in a mannerly fashion. They may pack different things depending on the trip — a suitcase to take on an airplane trip, or a picnic lunch to take on a boat ride. In planning the pretend trip, students may use the trip Questions/Comments Overlay, page 279, to ask about the trip. This may also be an opportunity to introduce a map, discussing parts of the country where we might travel.

Use the symbol vocabulary cards to allow students with limited physical or verbal ability to make choices about how we should travel.

Use the tune of "Row, row, row your boat" to sing about the trip. Change the words to go with the vehicle, e.g., "Fly, fly, fly the plane" or "Drive, drive, drive the car."

Use the suggestions in the Reading/Spelling Activities section, page 5, to create reading and spelling games with the words for this unit.

Several worksheets are included, pages 280-282, to help develop understanding of these vocabulary words. These may also be laminated and reused with Velcro® attached to the pictures.

This unit is a time to reinforce the town in which the student lives, helping them realize there are many other towns, also, with different names. A worksheet is included, page 283, for identification of the student's hometown, a friend (or relative) who lives in another town, and the method of transportation they would use to visit this other person.

Alphabetical Order

Two worksheets are included, pages 284 and 286, with letters in alphabetical order. The items on the accompanying overlays, pages 285 and 287, are grouped by categories, food items and toys. Depending on the student's ability level, they may be used to introduce alphabetizing or matching capital and small letters at the beginning of words. They may also be used as a simple sorting activity, separating the food items and toys.

Alphabetical Order (Cont.)

These pages may also be used for a sequential memory game. A student takes a turn stating the starter phrase, "I'm taking a trip and I will pack..." and names one item that they will pack. The next student will state the starter phrase, name the item that the previous student packed, and add another item. Visual cues may be included by adding the picture items on the worksheet as they are named. This is an activity that encourages students to take turns and attend to other students' responses.

An additional worksheet, Fly Me To The Sun!, is included, page 288, that allows the students to fill in the alphabet letters from A through P.

What Will You Pack?

Cut apart the category cards on page 289. Each student will take a turn packing an item for a trip. They will select a category card and name an item that belongs in this category. For some students, it may be necessary to have real items from these categories to select. Instruct the student to "find something to eat, a tool, a stuffed animal, etc."

Students using communication devices or books may have been creating "dictionary" sections with categories throughout other units (e.g., clothing items, food items, or animals). If not, this may be the time to include categorized dictionary sections.

The phrase "What will you pack?" may be used with a single switch device that enables students with limited physical abilities to ask other students what they will pack.

My Vacation

Encourage students to bring in photographs from a vacation they may have gone on. They may describe this vacation to the class. Students may ask questions about this trip. The trip Questions/Comments Overlay, page 279, can be used as a starter for who, what, where, and when questions. Students should also be encouraged to make comments about what the students have told of their vacations.

Aaron's Trip

The Aaron's Trip worksheet, page 290, describes a student's trip. Symbolized forms are included to encourage vocabulary recognition. It is also a means to incorporate time and money concepts. Students will add the hands to the clock and identify the coins needed on the worksheet.

The My Trip worksheet, page 291, is included so students may fill in about a trip. This might be used in conjunction with class field trips. Plan a trip to the park or a boat ride, or possibly visit an airport. Students will help in planning the trip, the time to go, and what they will need to pack. When completing the worksheet, include symbolized forms when possible. Students may also be able to type this information onto a computer. Or create an enlarged keyboard with word/sentence phrases.

This page could also be used to plan vacation trips. Students may select a place they would like to go. They may have to pack certain types of clothing, grooming items, etc. to go on this trip. Money may need to be taken for tickets or souvenirs. These simulated vacations may be shared with other students, giving them the opportunity to practice reading, time, and money skills.

Rider Safety

This unit is also a good opportunity to reinforce rider safety. Special emphasis should be placed on using a seat belt when riding in a car (see page 292). Other safety rules may be introduced, such as those pertaining to boats, buses, or bicycles.

Recreational Vehicles

Explore the different types of bicycles that this student may be able to ride. A bicycle shop may be able to loan a variety of tricycles, bicycles, or three-wheelers that can be ridden on the playground or a parking lot. Explore other riding toys that may be used with students who are in wheelchairs. Remember that helmets should be worn during these activities.

Additional Activity Sources

Units, "Transportation," Mayer-Johnson Co.

Taking A Trip

Level: Elementary

I want to take a trip.
Where will I go?
How will I get there?

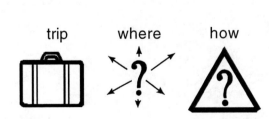

trip   where   how

Maybe I'll take a trip far, far away.
I'll go in an airplane.

trip 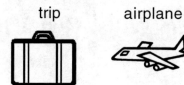 airplane

Level: Elementary

Zoom, zoom, zoom.
Fly in an airplane
far, far away.

fly airplane

Maybe I'll take a trip around a lake.
I'll go in a boat.

trip   boat

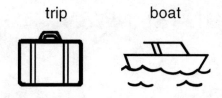

Level: Elementary

Row, row, row.
Row the boat
all around the lake.

row 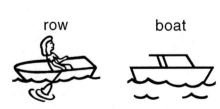 boat

Maybe I'll take a trip with my class.
I'll go in a bus.

trip   bus
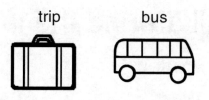

Level: Elementary

Bump, bump, bump.
Ride on a bus
with my class.

ride

bus

Maybe I'll take a trip to grandma's house.
I'll go in a car.

trip   car

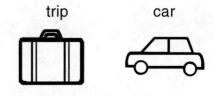

Level: Elementary

Beep, beep, beep.
Ride in a car
to grandma's house.

ride

car

Maybe I'll take a trip around the block.
I'll go on my bicycle.

trip

bicycle

Level: Elementary

I'll ride my bicycle around the block,
and pretend I'm on an airplane, a boat,
a car, and a bus!
What a fun trip I'll take!

fun

trip

Taking A Trip Overlay

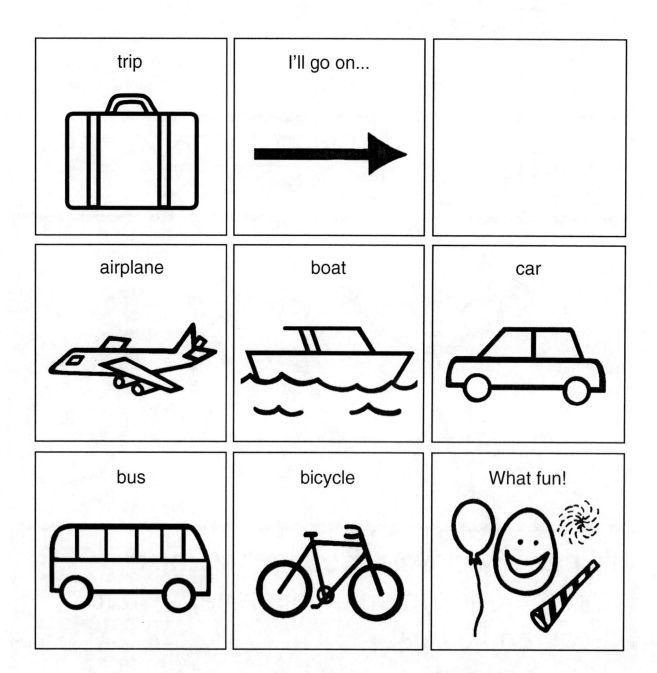

trip

I'll go on...

airplane

boat

car

bus

bicycle

What fun!

Level: Elementary

Vocabulary Cards (symbols)

airplane	car	bus	boat
bicycle	trip	ride	fly
row	go	pack	take
where	who	when	what
tractor	taxi	train	truck

Vocabulary Cards (words)

airplane	car	bus	boat
bicycle	trip	ride	fly
row	go	pack	take
where	who	when	what
tractor	taxi	train	truck

Level: Elementary

Questions/Comments Overlay

I have a question. 	Where did you go? 	How did you get there? 
Who did you go with? 	What did you do? 	Did you have fun? 
When did you go? 	Sounds great! 	Cool! 

Complete The Sentence

Cut out the picture symbols at the bottom of the page.
Glue them in the box next to the appropriate sentence.

I go in an airplane.

I go in a bus.

I go in a car.

I go in a boat.

I go on a bicycle.

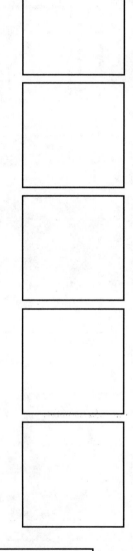

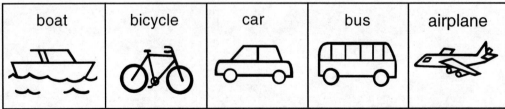

| boat | bicycle | car | bus | airplane |

Level: Elementary

Where Do They Belong?

Cut out the picture symbols at the bottom of the page. Glue them in the correct location.

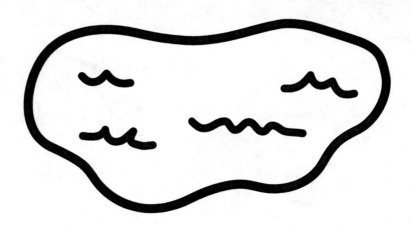

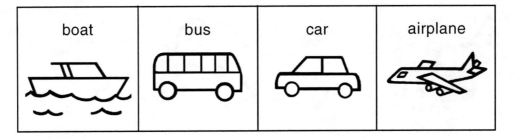

| boat | bus | car | airplane |

Things We Can Ride On

Circle the things we can ride on.

Level: Elementary

Where Do You Live?

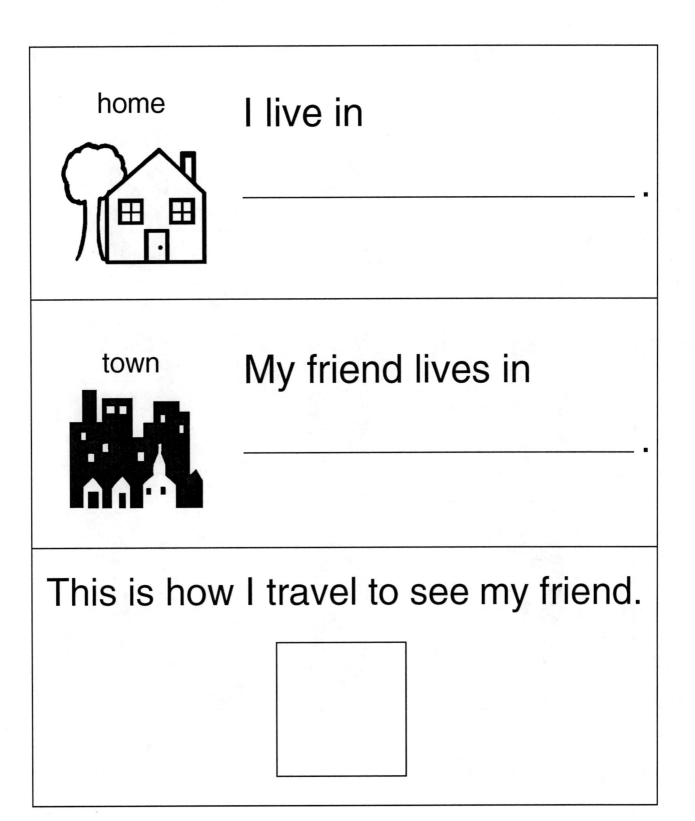

home

I live in

_____.

town

My friend lives in

_____.

This is how I travel to see my friend.

Alphabetical Order

Match the food items from page 285 that begin with each letter.

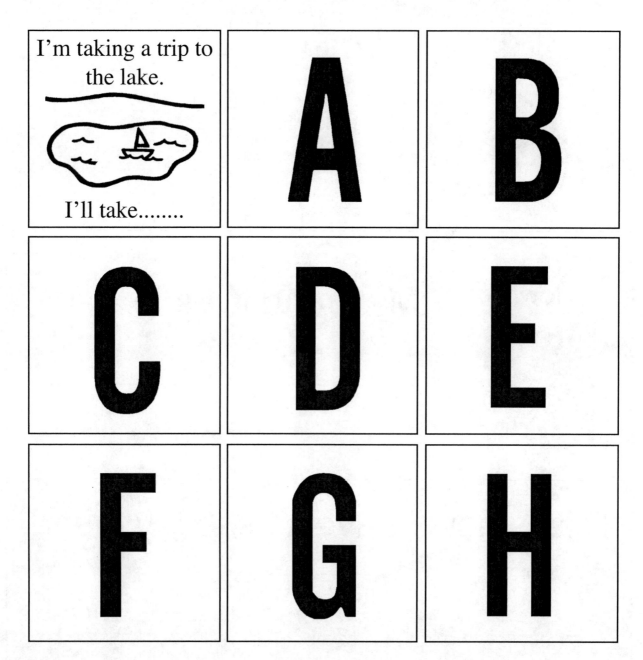

Food Items Overlay

apple

banana

chips

doughnut

egg

french fries

grapes

hot dog

Alphabetical Order

Match the toys from page 287 that begin with each letter.

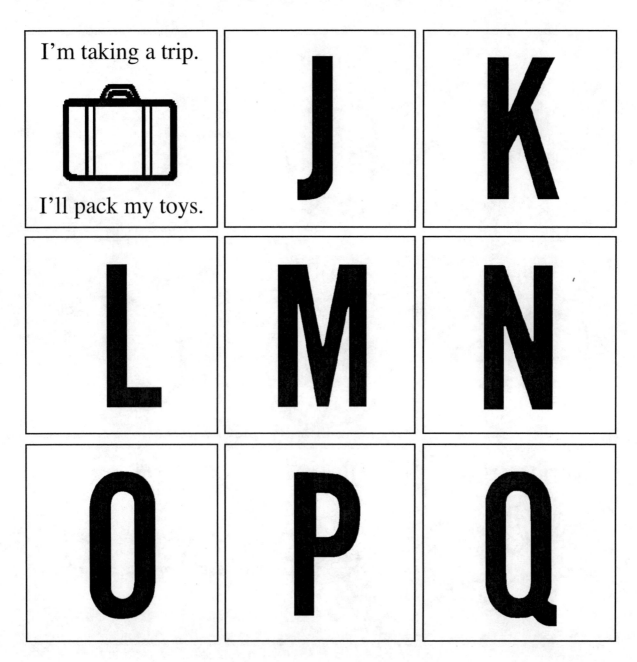

I'm taking a trip.

I'll pack my toys.

J

K

L

M

N

O

P

Q

Level: Elementary

Toys Overlay

	jump rope	kite
legoz	marbles	necklace
Oscar	puppet	queen

Fly Me To The Sun!

Fill in the letters from A to P.

Level: Elementary

What Will You Pack?

Cut apart the category cards.
Select a category; name items that belong in that category.

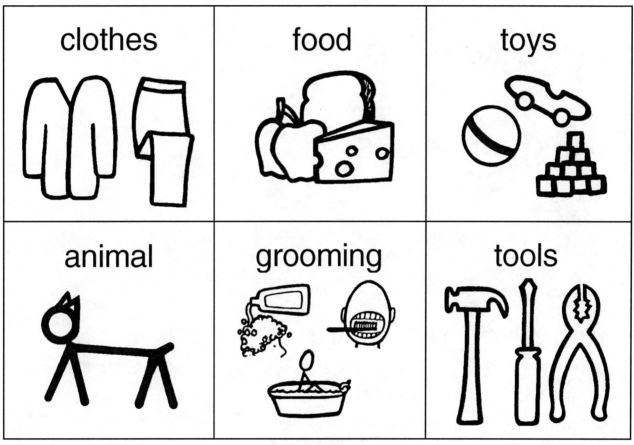

clothes

food

toys

animal

grooming

tools

Aaron's Trip

Draw the hands on the clock.
Identify the coins needed to buy a soda.

trip

I can take a trip.

bus

I will go in a bus.

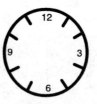

I will go at 9:00.

I will pack my lunch.
I pack a sandwich,
chips, and a banana.

sandwich   chips

banana

I bring $.50 to buy a
can of soda.

soda

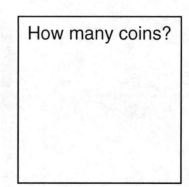

How many coins?

Level: Elementary

My Trip

Fill in the blanks and draw the hands on the clock.
Identify the coins needed to buy a drink.

trip

I can take a trip.

I will go in a _____ .

I will go at _____ .

I will pack

_____

_____ .

I bring _____ to buy a

_____ .

How many coins?

Seat Belt

When you ride,
put on your seat belt.

Level: Elementary

Name _____

Date _____

Unit Topic: Forest Animals

Literacy:
- ❑ demonstrates listening and attending behaviors during story reading
- ❑ participates in the story
- ❑ recognizes animals
- ❑ identifies animal homes
    - ❑ forest   ❑ zoo   ❑ farm
- ❑ recognizes basic sight words
- ❑ recognizes unit topic sight words
- ❑ applies decoding skills to words and sentences
- ❑ identifies numbers to 30

Communication:
- ❑ communicates during activities by _____
- ❑ expresses descriptive words related to senses
- ❑ responds to questions related to topic
- ❑ asks questions related to topic

Independent Living:
- ❑ identifies five senses
- ❑ recognizes personal reactions to senses

Community Living:
- ❑ identifies places where we can see animals
    - ❑ forest   ❑ zoo   ❑ farm
- ❑ demonstrates appropriate behavior in outdoor activities

Recreation/Leisure:
- ❑ participates in outdoor recreation activities
    - ❑ fishing   ❑ hiking
- ❑ demonstrates turn taking in group games

Vocational:
- ❑ works cooperatively in group activities
- ❑ has developed an awareness of jobs related to animal care

Level: Elementary

Forest Animals

forest

Dear Parents:

This new unit includes a story about taking a walk in the forest. During this story we will introduce the difference between forest and zoo animals. Many of our monthly activities will center around animals. We continue to present reading and math skills in all that we do.

Another aspect of this unit is learning about our senses — feeling, tasting, hearing, seeing, and smelling. Many students have a means to let us know what they like and don't like in reaction to their senses. This unit will attempt to increase vocabulary use in describing these feelings. Words like beautiful, yucky, delicious, and loud will be demonstrated in fun activities.

Sincerely,

Level: Elementary

The Story: A Walk In The Forest

This story, pages 299-310, involves children taking a walk in the forest and hoping to find some wild animals. As they progress, they hear sounds and try to guess what wild animal it might be. Then when they see what the animals is, it is a typical forest animal: squirrel, rabbit, raccoon, or fish. Descriptive words are used in describing these animals which might lead to discussion about how this animal might look or feel.

At the end of the story, the children remark that the next time they want to see wild animals they will go to the zoo. The story introduces the differences between forest and zoo animals.

The story repeats the actions of "listen" and "look." These actions are the tie to developing understanding of the five senses.

Suggested Vocabulary for Reading Activities

The Vocabulary Cards (symbols/words), pages 312 and 313, selected for this unit include forest and zoo animals, the five senses, and the body parts associated with these senses. These vocabulary words can be expanded through a variety of classroom and community experiences.

Differentiation between forest and zoo animals is explored by identifying where they live. Farm animals, which have been introduced in the primary level unit, may be added to this differentiation. Animal masks may be created for each student. Other students may ask the student what kind of animal they are, where they live, etc. Worksheets are included, pages 314-316, for sorting of these animals and their homes. These may also be laminated and used as a reusable sorting task.

Further expansion can be done by planning a hiking trip, field trip to a zoo, or fishing outing. Any of these trips would include a picnic lunch, which can be planned and packed by the students.

The vocabulary words also include the five senses: seeing with our eyes, feeling with our hands, tasting with our mouth, listening with our ears, and smelling with our nose. A worksheet is included, page 317.

As some students may have severe sensory impairments, this might also be an opportunity to discuss handicapping conditions and how they affect us. Sometimes, when a sensory impairment is present, presentation of information through these channels is limited. The activities in this unit may increase our awareness of how to stimulate the residual use of impaired senses.

Use the suggestions in the Reading/Spelling Activities section, page 5, to create reading and spelling games with the words for this unit. Fish patterns are included, page 318. The vocabulary words/symbols may be glued to these patterns to make a fishing game with a magnet pole and paper clips attached to the patterns.

Math Counting Activities

A worksheet is included, page 319, for sequencing numbers to 25. These may be written or number cards can be glued onto each space.

Students with limited physical ability should be encouraged to use alternate modes to tell what number is next.

A variety of counting activities may be added to this unit. Duplicate animal pictures for counting or adding. Ask the students how many animals are in the forest, how many they can catch, how many are in the cage, etc.

My Pet

Pets may be related to the animals of this unit. A worksheet is included, page 320, for the students to complete about their own pets. A special pet day may be arranged where the parents bring the pet in for a "pet show." This is also a good opportunity to encourage the students to ask questions of the other students (e.g., "What kind of pet do you have?" "What is your pet's name?"). Pets may also be described using the senses of seeing, hearing, and feeling:

- What color is it?
- Is it big or little?
- How does it feel?
- Does the pet make a sound?
- Is it a loud or quiet pet?

Our Senses

If we are to use our senses, we must have descriptive words that tell what we see, hear, feel, taste, or smell. This unit should provide experiences where the students can learn and use these descriptive words.

Almost all reactions to a stimuli can be expressed as good or bad, differentiating things we like or don't like. However, the way we communicate these likes and dislikes can be very different. Some students may have a facial or body reaction that tells us how they feel about something. Others may have vocalizations while some have a physical reaction, such as throwing objects that are undesirable. In the classroom activities, we must be able to "read" these natural reactions and strive to present the students with descriptive vocabulary which serves as a more appropriate and sophisticated means to relate these feelings.

Descriptive cards are included, pages 321-323, with typical descriptive words that are used when smelling, hearing, looking, feeling, and tasting. During stimulating activities, these words should be made available to the student. For example, the student smiles when tasting chocolate pudding. The facilitator will present the card and model, "It tastes delicious." Or the student covers his/her ears when hearing loud music. The facilitator will present the card and model, "That sound is too loud. We'll turn it down."

Make note of the nonspeech modes that students use to express these descriptors and what picture symbols are used to model these feelings. A blank card is included at the bottom of page 323 that will allow each student to have a customized descriptor board. This can serve as their own personal model for use at any time during the day. Verbal students with language limitations may also use this to help them discriminate their use of descriptors.

It is wise to discuss etiquette in using negative descriptors. For example, it is not wise to tell the school cook that the meal was "yucky."

Ideas for Stimulating Use of the Senses

Tasting Party
A variety of food choices may be included each day during snack time. Include various tastes and textures.

Mighty Milkshakes
Make vanilla milkshakes using a blender. Add flavoring to small portions, such as strawberry, banana, coconut, etc. Students will first smell the milkshake and decide on one to try. After selecting one, they may drink it. This will add use of smelling and tasting descriptors.

Petting Party
Present a variety of textures to feel, e.g., stuffed animals, sandpaper, ice, cotton balls, slime, etc. Students will take turns feeling an item and describing how it feels.

Baking Cookies
Prepare and bake cookies with a distinct smell. Describe the dough, the cookies as they bake, and how they taste when done. Use as many senses as possible in this activity.

A Sock Hop
Bring in different types of music tapes or records: country, rock, inspirational, etc. Play different songs for an afternoon sock hop. If the student likes the music, they may dance. If they don't, they can sit it out. Explore different volumes.

Clothes Shopping
Look through catalogs or flyers to pick new clothes. Describe the ones that are likes/dislikes using the descriptor cards. Cut out the clothes that are desirable. Share their choices with the other students. This is when etiquette comes into play— students should offer a comment that is positive, i.e. "It looks great" or "It looks beautiful."

Additional Activity Sources

Units, "Animals," Mayer-Johnson Co.

Hands-on Reading, "Animal Unit," Mayer-Johnson Co.

I Can Cook, Too!, "Zoo Crackers, Jurassic Pudding," Mayer-Johnson Co.

Interactive Augmentative Communication Program, "Texture Game," page 196, and "Our Pet Fish," page 278, Mayer-Johnson Co.

Level: Elementary

A Walk In The Forest

Let's take a walk, a walk in the forest.
Will I find wild animals hiding from me?

walk   forest    animals   hide

Level: Elementary

Listen, I hear something up in the tree.
Is it a monkey or maybe a lion?

listen   monkey   lion

Look, it's a fluffy gray squirrel nibbling on a nut.

look  squirrel

Level: Elementary

Listen, I hear something under the flowers.
Is it an elephant or maybe a bear?

listen   elephant   bear

Look, it's a soft white rabbit wiggling his nose.

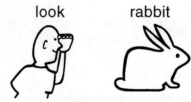

look   rabbit

Level: Elementary

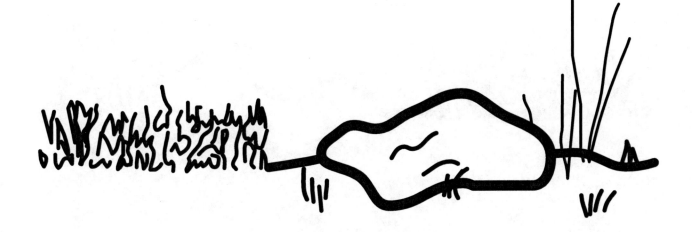

Listen, I hear something behind the rock.
Is it a kangaroo or maybe a zebra?

listen   kangaroo   zebra

Look, it's a small brown raccoon digging a hole.

look   raccoon

Listen, I hear something down in the pond.
Is it an alligator or maybe a whale?

listen   alligator   whale

Look, it's a slippery goldfish
blowing bubbles in the water.

look   fish

Level: Elementary

We went for a walk, a walk in the forest.

walk forest

But next time I want to find wild animals,
I'll go to the zoo!

animals   zoo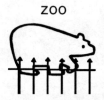

Level: Elementary

A Walk In The Forest Overlay

Walk in the forest.	Listen, I hear...	Look, I see...
wild animals	squirrel	rabbit
raccoon	fish	I'll go to the zoo.

Vocabulary Cards (symbols)

squirrel	raccoon	rabbit	fish
monkey	lion	elephant	zebra
look	listen	smell	taste
touch	eyes	ear	hand
mouth	nose	good	bad

Level: Elementary

Vocabulary Cards (words)

squirrel	raccoon	rabbit	fish
monkey	lion	elephant	zebra
look	listen	smell	taste
touch	eyes	ear	hand
mouth	nose	good	bad

Complete The Sentence

Cut out the picture symbols at the bottom of the page.
Glue them in the box next to the appropriate sentence.

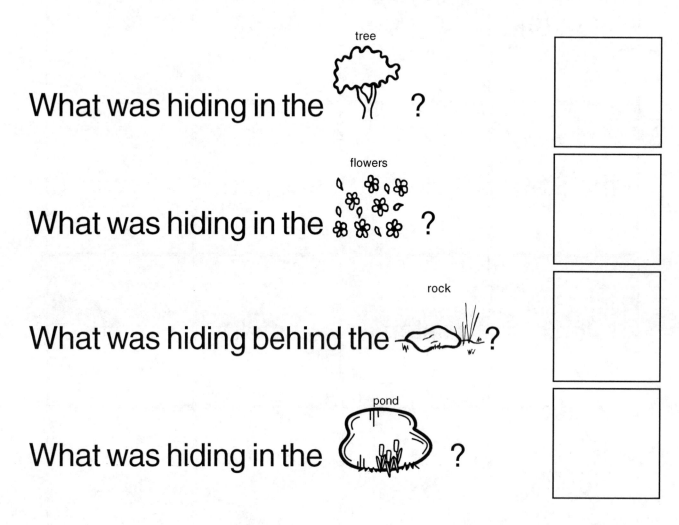

tree

What was hiding in the 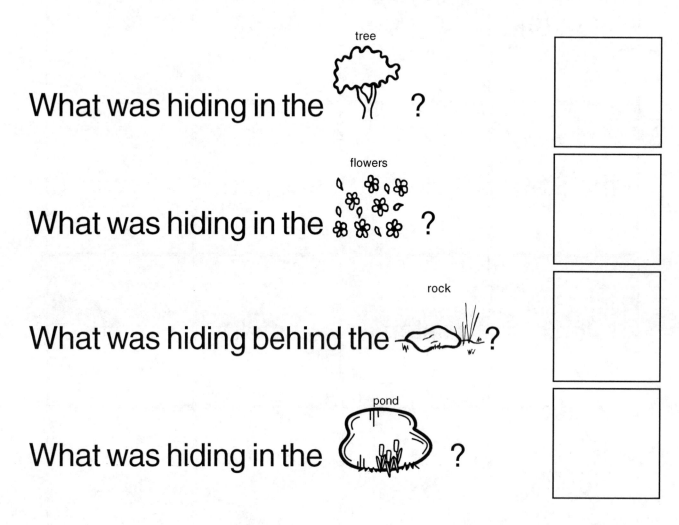 ?

flowers

What was hiding in the ?

rock

What was hiding behind the ?

pond

What was hiding in the ?

fish 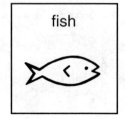	rabbit 	raccoon 	squirrel 

Level: Elementary

Where Do They Live?

Cut out the picture symbols at the bottom of the page. Glue them under the appropriate category.

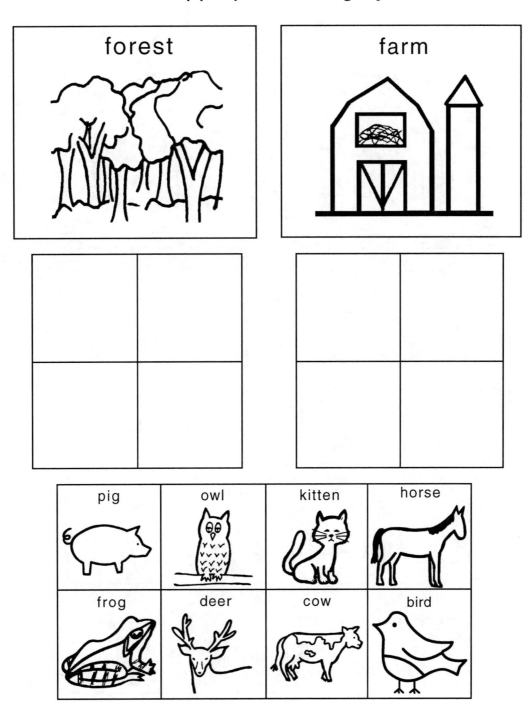

Where Do They Live?

Cut out the picture symbols at the bottom of the page.
Glue them under the appropriate category.

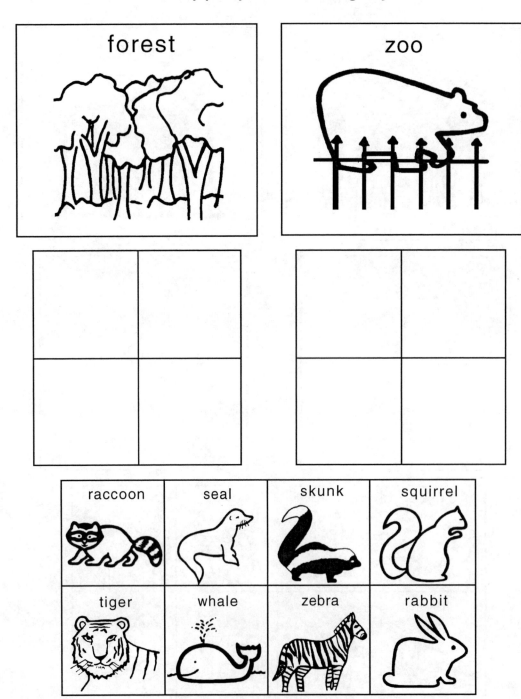

Level: Elementary

Matching

Cut out the picture symbols at the bottom of the page.
Match the five senses.

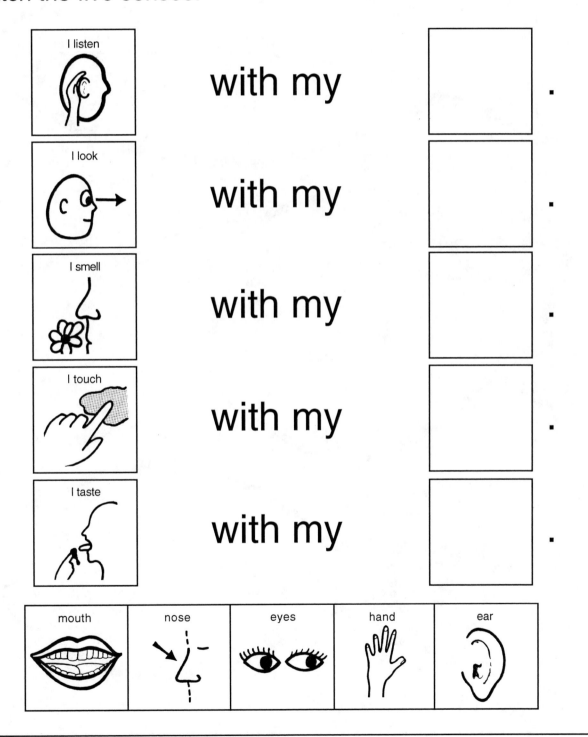

Fish Patterns

Level: Elementary

Help Squirrel Find The Nuts

Fill in the numbers from 1 to 25.

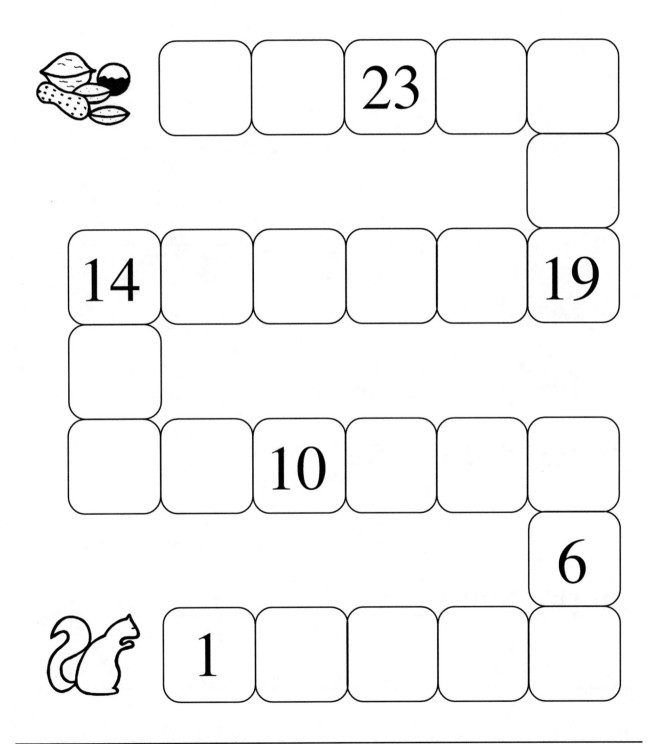

My Pet

Glue a picture of your pet here.

My pet is a _____.

My pet's name is _____.

My pet likes to eat _____

_____.

My pet lives_____

_____.

Level: Elementary

Descriptive Cards

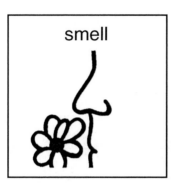

It smells....

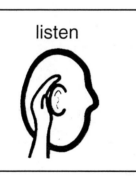

It sounds....

Descriptive Cards

It looks....

good	delicious	great	beautiful	new
bad	yucky	silly	messy	wrong

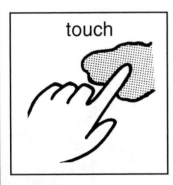

It feels....

good	smooth	soft	nice	cold
bad	rough	gross	sticky	hot

Level: Elementary

Descriptive Cards

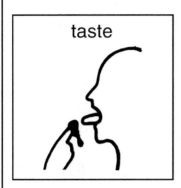

taste

It tastes....

| good | delicious | sweet | crunchy | too cold |
| bad | yucky | spicy | sour | too hot |

Make your own.

It looks.....	It smells.....	It sounds.....	It feels.....	It tastes.....
good				
bad				